Trees & Shrubs of Washington

LONE PINE

C.P. Lyons

The Publisher: Lone Pine Publishing

206, 10426–81 Avenue	202A, 1110 Seymour Street	1901 Raymond Avenue SW, Suite C
Edmonton, AB T6E 1X5	Vancouver, BC V6B 3N3	Renton, WA 98055
Canada	Canada	USA

Lone Pine Publishing website: http://www.lonepinepublishing.com

Canadian Cataloguing in Publication Data

Lyons, C. P. (Chester Peter), 1915–98
    Trees and shrubs of Washington

    Includes bibliographical references and index.
    ISBN 1-55105-094-3

    1. Trees—Washington (State)—Identification. 2. Shrubs—Washington (State)—Identification. I. Title.
QK192.L962 1999   582' .16'09797   C99-910384-9

Editorial Director: Nancy Foulds
Production Manager: Jody Reekie
Editorial: Volker Bodegom, Erin McCloskey, Lee Craig
Layout & Production: Michelle Bynoe
Book Design: Michelle Bynoe, Robert Weidemann
Cover Design: Michelle Bynoe
Cover Photo: Grove of giant cedars and hemlocks by Graham Osborne
Separations & Film: Elite Lithographers Ltd.
Photography: All photographs are by the author and Bill Merilees.
Ilustrations: All illustrations are by the author except crack willow p. 42 and p. 73: illustration by A. Meriolle in *North American Trees* (by Nathaniel Lord Britton, 1908).

Although this guide mentions medicinal and culinary uses of plants, it is not a 'how-to' reference for using traditional plant-derived medicines or foods. We do not recommend experimentation by readers, and we caution that many plants in our region, including some with traditional medical or food use—or look-alikes—can be poisonous or harmful.

We acknowledge the financial support of the Government of Canada through the Book Publishing Industry Development Program (BPIDP) for our publishing activities.

PC: P4   Canadä

CONTENTS

PREFACE

Chess Lyons seemed delighted when work began in earnest on this book, part of a proposed series of books for Washington and British Columbia. He had spent the last few years collecting information and photos for *Wildflowers of Washington* (1997) and this book.

Chess telephoned every month or so to check on the progress of whatever book was in the works and to keep us posted on his upcoming jaunts to Washington to photograph plants or more ambitious trips to Morocco, or Iceland, or Bali, or some other amazing corner of the globe. Along the way we learned about his garden in Victoria and the pleasure it gave him. He revelled in knowing that we were snowbound in the middle of a prairie winter while he was out and about in shirtsleeves.

Chess died suddenly in Hawaii on December 20, 1998. He was in his early 80s. Always active and determined in his endeavors, he was nevertheless a modest man who never mentioned his many accomplishments unless he was asked about them. His legacy began with his involvement with the fledgling BC Parks in 1940 and in countless other ways. His greatest contribution, however, lies in his much-loved field guides to the plants of the Pacific Northwest, beginning in 1952 with the publication of *Trees, Shrubs and Flowers to Know in British Columbia.* Chess's books have informed and inspired several generations of naturalists and foresters as they walked the forests and meadows of Washington and British Columbia.

Chess's death came at a time when this book was still in production here at Lone Pine. It would seem fitting to finish up without him, knowing that through the book Chess can continue to expand the minds of readers. We are grateful for the contributions of Andy MacKinnon and Bill Merilees, who generously helped out with the later stages of this book.

Nancy Foulds
Volker Bodegom
Lone Pine Publishing

ACKNOWLEDGMENTS

Trees and Shrubs of Washington is adapted from my original flora book, *Trees, Shrubs and Flowers to Know in Washington* (1956), and the major revision that I made over several years with the help of Bill Merilees, *Trees, Shrubs and Flowers to Know in Washington and British Columbia* (1995). This newest guide adds color photographs of most plants and references to the travels and collections of Archibald Menzies, Lewis and Clark, and David Douglas. I hope that being able to relate the early explorers to some of the flora of Washington will lead to a better appreciation of these early endeavors. There is still a thrill of discovery yourself when you chance for the first time to find a flowering tree in a forest glade or a colorful shrub high on a mountainside.

Bill Merilees has helped with photos from his extensive collection. Ruth Kirk has advised on organization and descriptions, and Ernie McNaughton has checked for botanical accuracy. Trish Ellison tackled transcribing my abominably written notes into computer format. Volker Bodegom, an editor at Lone Pine Publishing, has helped me to clarify and embellish my writing beyond what I would have managed otherwise. However, I take full responsibility for all aberrations. To these people and others who have helped in various ways, your efforts have been much appreciated.

INTRODUCTION

EXPLORER-BOTANISTS

Most pioneer botanists would also qualify as explorers. Their travels into the wilderness often involved considerable personal danger. Clothes, food and equipment were unbelievably scant, yet the lure of new country and undiscovered flora led them forward. Fortunately their names live on, often commemorated in the names of plants. (Note: There are detailed notes on the Lewis and Clark Expedition and David Douglas's travels and collections in my companion volume, *Wildflowers of Washington* [Lone Pine Publishing, 1997].)

William Anderson • 1750–78

William Anderson was surgeon/botanist on James Cook's third voyage, which arrived in Nootka Sound in 1778. When he made the first known collections of plants for northwestern America, the science of classifying and naming plants was only 25 years old! Unfortunately, Anderson was quite ill at the time and died shortly thereafter, leaving to others the task of collecting and naming West Coast flora.

Archibald Menzies • 1754–1842

On Captain George Vancouver's voyage to the west coast of North America, Archibald Menzies was the expedition's surgeon and botanist. His instructions were 'to investigate the whole of the natural history of the countries visited.' As Menzies came ashore in May 1792 at Port Discovery, his was the first scientific mind to fully appreciate the natural wonders, such as the

Menzies '...impenetrable stretches of pinery....' He made an excursion into the woods '...and met...a beautiful shrub *Rhododendron ponticum*,'—now the state flower of Washington and known as Pacific rhododendron, *R. macrophyllum*.

Meriwether Lewis • 1774–1809
William Clark • 1770–1838

The adventurous Lewis and Clark Expedition of 1804–06, which traveled across western North America to the Pacific Ocean, receives more and more acclaim with the passing years. Sir Alexander Mackenzie had traversed Canada to the Pacific Ocean in 1793. He had proposed the 45th parallel as the U.S.–Canada border, which would have secured for Britain an

Clark

ocean port at the Columbia River. Thomas Jefferson, the U.S. president at the time, felt it was imperative that an exploration of the far west be carried out before the British laid claim to the land.

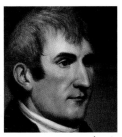

Among the wide scope of Lewis and Clark's duties of recording '...objects worthy of notice' were '...the soil and face of the country, its growth and vegetable production.' Among Lewis' supplies was a book, *Barton's Elements of Botany*, and a large package of purple blotting paper for pressing plant spec-

Lewis

imens. Despite the daily hazards of travel, both men collected not only plants but other aspects of natural history. They kept careful notes and often made detailed drawings.

Lewis and Clark found 178 plants then unknown to Europeans. Two-thirds of these plants were found west of the Rocky Mountains. Their collections were examined by Frederick Pursh, a European botanist who was living in Philadelphia while he worked on a flora of North America. He gave scientific names to many of their plants. Various plants, particularly the flowers, show their association with the explorers in their names. One beautiful shrub that Lewis collected was mock-orange, *Philadelphus lewisii*.

David Douglas • 1799–1834

This adventurous young Scotsman roamed a vast wilderness encompassing much of present-day Oregon, Washington and British Columbia. He recorded many new plant species and introduced no fewer than 254 plants to Great Britain. The wide-ranging Douglas-fir tree was named after him. His journals provide an intriguing glimpse of his thoughts about the flora and conditions relating to his travels.

David Douglas had already botanized on behalf of the Royal Horticultural Society of London in 1823 in the northeastern United States and Canada. When the Horticultural Society and the Hudson's Bay Company wanted to explore an area of wilderness on the Pacific Northwest Coast, Douglas was proposed for the project. His ship landed near the mouth of the Columbia River on April 17, 1825.

Douglas was quickly on the go and learned the skills of water and woods travel. His interests went far beyond the field of botany, for he collected birds, animals and other aspects of natural history. In fact, he was an outstanding all-round naturalist. By the end of 1825, he estimated that he had covered 3388 km (2105 mi). The fever of wilderness travel and collecting was in his blood, and the next year he recorded traveling 6400 km (4000 mi). The following year was even more strenuous for, in an unbelievable journey, he took the fur trade route northward through British Columbia and traveled over 1600 km (1000 mi) to a fort on Hudson Bay, and then sailed to England.

There, he soon tired of the adulation and the formidable task of compiling his notes. He eagerly accepted an assignment to return to the Pacific Northwest and also to botanize in California. After a long voyage, he arrived in Fort Vancouver on October 31, 1829, and made his way southward to California. When he returned to Fort Vancouver on June 3, 1833, he was eager to start a dream he

Douglas

had long had in mind: to travel, mostly by foot, to Britain via a southerly route through Russia. He made a start and covered about 1900 km (1200 mi) to reach Fort St. James in remote northern British Columbia. Beyond were so many obstacles that he abandoned his dream. He backtracked to the Fraser River at Prince George and launched a canoe, only to be upset in the nearby rapids and nearly drown—a serious blow in that he lost his specimens and precious journal. Then it was 1450 km (900 mi) of travel back to Fort Vancouver. Shortly afterward, he had a chance to travel to the Sandwich (Hawaiian) Islands. While on the Big Island of Hawaii, he fell into a pit dug to trap wild cattle and was gored to death by a trapped bull. Douglas was only 35 years old when he died, but in that short lifetime he made a major contribution to the world's knowledge of Northwest flora. Could he not be classed as the world's most enthusiastic botanist?

Douglas: 'It is a barren place that does not afford me a blade of grass, a bird or a rock...from which I can derive an expressable delight.'

Sir William Hooker • 1785–1865

It was William Hooker who supported and advanced David Douglas's career as an explorer/collector for the Royal Horticultural Society of London. Also, as the recipient of much of the material that Douglas collected, it was Hooker who described and published many of the results.

Thomas Nuttall • 1786–1859

What greater tribute might be paid to an explorer than to have western flowering dogwood, *Cornus nuttallii*, named for him? Thomas Nuttall was a 'botanical explorer' who ventured into many areas of western North America. In addition, he named many plants collected by other botanists. Nuttall was professor of natural history at Harvard University from 1822–34.

John Scouler, M.D. • 1804–71

John Scouler was appointed geologist/surgeon/naturalist on the William and Mary, the ship that carried David Douglas to the mouth of the Columbia River on his first trip to the Pacific Northwest in 1825. It was Scouler's only trip of note.

Sir Joseph Hooker • 1817–1911

The son of Sir William, above, Sir Joseph Hooker was renowned as one of the most colorful and talented botanists in Europe. Early in his career he collected plants in the Rocky Mountains.

David Lyall, M.D. • 1817–95

During the International Boundary Survey of 1858–60, David Lyall reported the occurrence of the subalpine larch, subsequently named *Larix lyalli*, along the 49th parallel. Lyall had previously served as a surgeon in the Royal Navy during the North American coastal surveys of Captain George Richards.

THE ECOSYSTEMS

San Juan Islands

The San Juan Islands lie between the southern tip of Vancouver Island and mainland Washington. South-facing lands with grassy slopes feature arbutus and Garry oak. In protected areas, a rich mixture of broadleaf and evergreen trees adds more variety and color. These islands are world-famous for their mild climate and low precipitation, as a result of being in the rainshadow of the Olympic Mountains. The average annual rainfall is 75 cm (30") and snow is unusual.

Coast Forest

The name 'coast forest' is used in the broadest sense to cover forests on the Pacific side of the Cascades up to subalpine elevations. A more complex classification would see a division at around 1200 m (4000'), where lowland coastal species are replaced by mountain hemlock, amabilis fir, subalpine fir and yellow-cedar. Coastal rainfall often averages 200 cm (79") per year. Winters are mild, but at higher elevations temperatures are lower and there is considerably more snow.

Subalpine

Above the dense coastal forests, this subalpine region of green glades, picturesque trees and expansive meadows is backed by magnificent mountain scenery. It draws millions of visitors each year to the Olympics, Mt. Baker and Mt. Rainier. Hikers can reach less well-known areas, such as Mt. Shuksan and Mt. St. Helens. The Blue Mountains have high ridges in the subalpine. Winters are long and severe, and snow accumulates to great depths. Open terrain and deep snow create ideal conditions for ski resorts.

Alpine Tundra

The name 'alpine tundra' is replacing the more common term 'alpine.' But where is the division between the subalpine and the alpine tundra? The matter is not as simple as saying 'timberline,' for stunted trees creep high up some mountains. The boundary where the rich growth of grasses and flowers gives way to near-barren rocky slopes and

ridges is more discernible. There the rockery plants take over: the heathers, dwarf willows, moss campions and saxifrages.

This change-over occurs at about 1350 m (4400') on southern coastal mountains and at about 1800 m (5900') east of the Cascades. Weather conditions are severe, with long winters and short summers. Access by mountain roads and helicopters makes the alpine tundra a spectacular setting for winter sports.

Mountain Forest

Like the coast forest ecosystem, the mountain forest ecosystem also has several arbitrary divisions. As you enter it by descending from the subalpine, it consists almost entirely of white spruce, Engelmann spruce and subalpine fir. As you move lower, there is a transition to lodgepole pine, larch, cottonwood and birch. Engelmann spruce continues into these lower elevations. The bulk of this ecosystem lies on the eastern slopes of the Cascades, but other such areas are found at higher elevations in northeastern Washington, such as within the Okanogan and Colville national forests and also on the northern slopes of the Blue Mountains.

Ponderosa Pine

The ponderosa pine ecosystem is easily identified by the presence of these beautiful pines—growing either in pure, open stands or mixed with Douglas-fir—up to an elevation as high as 1050 m (3500'), where this ecosystem is replaced by the mountain forest ecosystem. A strip of ponderosa pine ecosystem extends northward from about the mid-point of the Columbia Gorge, through Klickitat, Kittitas and Chelan counties to the hillsides of the Okanogan Valley. It is also common north, south and east of Spokane. The climate is extremely arid, with hot summer days and freezing winter temperatures. Annual rainfall is 25–50 cm (10–20").

Bunchgrass

The bunchgrass ecosystem classification takes in the terrain between the lower edge of the ponderosa pine ecosystem and the upper border of the sagebrush ecosystem. This ecosystem can be described as occupying over one-half of the part of the state east of the Cascade Range and south of a line connecting Brewster and Spokane, with extensions northward into British Columbia along the Okanogan Valley. However, except along the Okanogan Valley, much of this ecosystem has been converted into an interlocking grid of farms. Its elevation range is generally 450–750 m (1500–2400'), though it can reach 900 m (3000') in some tributary valleys. Extremely hot summers contrast with cold winters. Snow to a depth of 30–60 cm (1–2') covers the ground for several months each year.

Sagebrush

The sagebrush ecosystem coincides with the most arid regions of the state. Its boundaries are often quite obvious. Although there are usually several shrubs other than sagebrush, nearly all have a 'sagebrushy' color and form. This ecosystem covers a large part of the Columbia Plateau, and a wide arm branches along the Yakima River toward

Cle Elum. Another strip borders the Columbia River from Pasco westward to The Dalles, and there is a strip that borders the Snake River. It is also prominent as you follow the Okanogan Valley and U.S. Route 97 northward to B.C. Tributary valleys carry it to approximately 700 m (2300') in elevation. Streams, ponds, marshes and coulees are part of this landscape, and their small but special habitats make a wide variety of flora possible. The summer heat is intense, winters see freezing temperatures and the annual rainfall is less than 25 cm (10").

Interior Cedar-Hemlock

The extent of the interior cedar–hemlock ecosystem is difficult to define because it is greatly influenced by river courses and adjoining mountain slopes. It tends to form north–south strips and pockets largely at 600–1500 m (2000–5000') in elevation. These areas are southward projections from fairly extensive forests in British Columbia. The yellow-green fronds of redcedar provide the easiest identification. Western hemlock is quite scarce. There is an easy melding with larch, spruce, lodgepole pine, white pine, Douglas-fir, aspen, birch and cottonwoods.

The valleys of the Pend Oreille River and its tributaries north of Tiger contain the bulk of this ecosystem. A stand of giant redcedar once stood at Sullivan Lake before it was flooded. Highway 31 is flanked by redcedar for 16 km (10 mi) south of the British Columbia border. The rather heavy precipitation of 50–100 cm (20–40") is caused by clouds losing their moisture as they climb the windward side of high mountain systems.

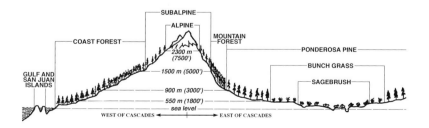

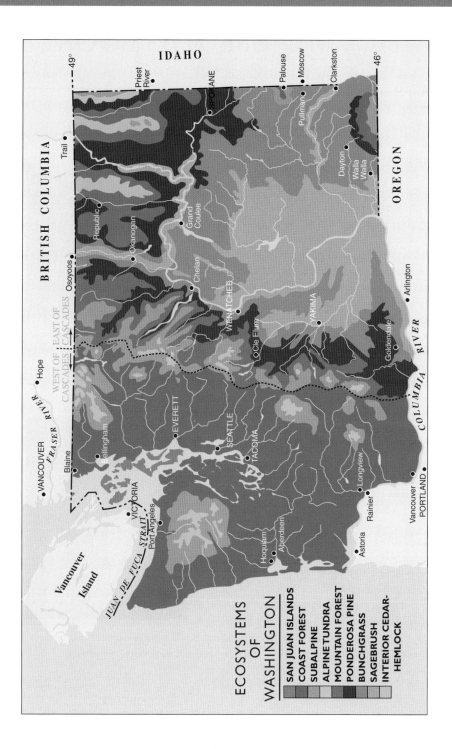

ECOSYSTEMS
OF
WASHINGTON

SAN JUAN ISLANDS
COAST FOREST
SUBALPINE
ALPINE TUNDRA
MOUNTAIN FOREST
PONDEROSA PINE
BUNCHGRASS
SAGEBRUSH
INTERIOR CEDAR-
HEMLOCK

IDAHO

BRITISH COLUMBIA

OREGON

Priest River
SPOKANE
Palouse
Moscow
Clarkston
Pullman
Trail
Dayton
Walla Walla
Republic
Okanogan
Grand Coulee
Osoyoos
Chelan
WENATCHEE
Arlington
YAKIMA
Cle Elum
Goldendale
Hope
COLUMBIA RIVER
WEST OF
EAST OF
CASCADES CASCADES
FRASER RIVER
VANCOUVER
EVERETT
SEATTLE
TACOMA
Bellingham
Blaine
VICTORIA
Port Angeles
Longview
Rainier
Vancouver
PORTLAND
Hoquiam
Aberdeen
Astoria
JUAN DE FUCA STRAIT
Vancouver
Island

49°
46°

13

HOW TO USE THIS BOOK

A Tree or a Shrub?

Trees have strong trunks covered in bark. They are usually over 6 m (20') tall, with trunks more than 5 cm (2") in diameter. In general, a tree has a single trunk. A major division is into evergreen trees, usually with needles, and broadleaf trees, usually with deciduous leaves. There are two special cases of broadleaf trees— arbutus and California wax-myrtle—with leaves that persist all year. In addition, western and subalpine larch, both classed as evergreens, look 'evergreen' during spring and summer but drop their needles in late autumn.

Often a plant's habitat dictates whether it forms a tree or shrub. Here, shrubs and trees are grouped with related species. For example, the alders, maples and cherries can be compared easily if all members of each family are considered as trees.

An attempt has been made to group together related evergreen trees or those with a common habitat. The same applies to broadleaf trees. See p. 17 and p. 47 for the two keys to the trees.

Shrubs have several tough, woody stems covered in bark. Generally, they are under 6 m (20') tall and the trunks are less than 5 cm (2") in diameter. A slender tree in a shady valley bottom could be the same species as a shrubby growth on a nearby rocky hillside. A proper key to the shrubs would have to use floral features, which are beyond the scope of this book. Merely grouping by flower colors would only lead to confusion because of so many similarities. Fruits vary greatly and are often difficult to describe.

Therefore, the 'List of Shrubs' on p. 83 attempts a rough grouping according to form or habitat. A given shrub might well fit under several headings, but is listed just once. A quick inspection of a specimen might provide a clue to a name and its position in the book.

What Is in a Name?

Scientific (or Latin, or botanical) names are designed to be consistent throughout the world, but common names are often a matter of local usage. The scientific name is usually in two parts, like a person's. The following chart shows how a comparison might be made. In the example, *Pinus* is the **genus** (plural 'genera') and *ponderosa* identifies the particular **species**.

Anglo-Saxon (a clan of people)	Pinaceae (a 'clan' of trees)
Smith, Clark (families in the clan)	*Pinus, Larix, Abies* ('families'in the 'clan')
William Smith (a specific person)	*Pinus ponderosa* (a specific pine tree species)

The following abbreviations are also used:

spp. = species: Used with a genus name (e.g., *Larix* spp.) to mean several species or all species in that genus.

ssp. = subspecies: Used after a species name (e.g., *Populus balsamifera* ssp. *trichocarpa*) to indicate a finer division of the species, often corresponding to its geographical range.

var. = variety: Used the same way as **ssp.** (e.g., *Pinus contorta* var. *latifolia*), though typically used to distinguish plants with a common range but slightly different characteristics (e.g., in leaf or flower).

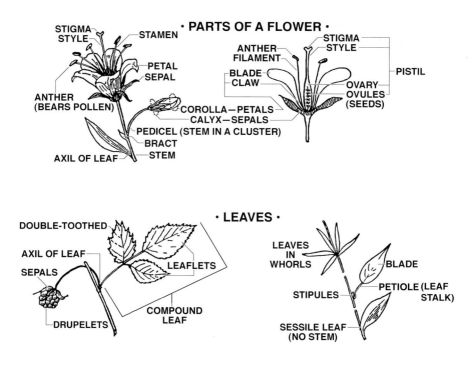

· PARTS OF A FLOWER ·

· LEAVES ·

KEY TO EVERGREEN TREES

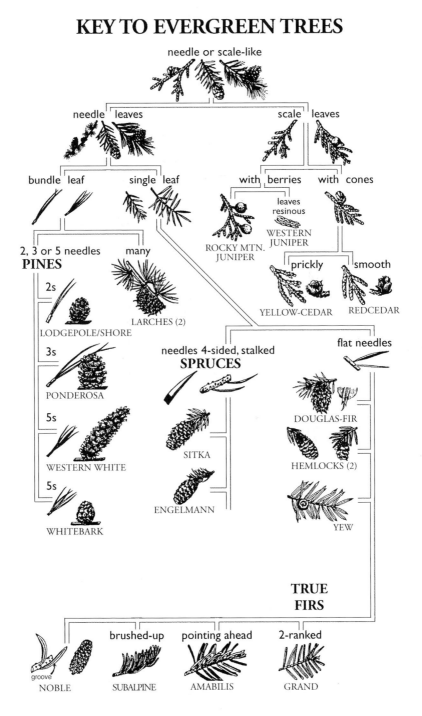

needle or scale-like

needle leaves   scale leaves

bundle leaf   single leaf   with berries   with cones

2, 3 or 5 needles   many
PINES

leaves resinous
WESTERN JUNIPER
ROCKY MTN. JUNIPER

prickly   smooth

2s

LARCHES (2)

LODGEPOLE/SHORE

YELLOW-CEDAR   REDCEDAR

flat needles

3s

needles 4-sided, stalked
SPRUCES

PONDEROSA

DOUGLAS-FIR

5s

SITKA

WESTERN WHITE

HEMLOCKS (2)

5s

ENGELMANN

WHITEBARK

YEW

TRUE FIRS

groove
brushed-up   pointing ahead   2-ranked

NOBLE   SUBALPINE   AMABILIS   GRAND

17

DOUGLAS-FIR
Pseudotsuga menziesii

Possibly the most impressive, important and widespread tree in western North America. Found near mouth of Columbia River by Archibald Menzies in 1792. He later named it after explorer-botanist David Douglas.

'Pitchfork' bracts on cones provide definite identification. And there are always cones on the ground. Most mature trees on the coast are 0.9–1.2 m (3–4') in diameter and 60 m (200') tall. Some giants remain—to 4 m (13') in diameter, near 90 m (300') tall and possibly 1400 years old. Bark is deeply furrowed.

The first recorded mention of the trees of the Pacific Coast was by Captain James Cook, who in 1778 was at Nootka on the west coast of Vancouver Island. The masts of his ships were rotting and were replaced with Douglas-fir. Never before could a mast that size be replaced by a single tree. Previously, 2 trees had been spliced together to make 1 mast.

Before chainsaws became common equipment, felling axes, long cross-cut saws, wedges and 'turp' bottles (turpentine, to counteract pitch) were standard tools for loggers. The fallers cut deep notches above the brush and butt-swell, and drove in metal-tipped springboards on which to stand. A saw cut was made into the tree and then a huge wedge of wood chopped out. It could take a day of hard toil to fell one of these forest giants.

Millions of Douglas-fir Christmas trees are cut in Washington and shipped abroad each year. Large freighters unload at Honolulu and others go to more distant destinations.

As with all prominent plants, Native American peoples had many uses for the Douglas-fir. Its resinous wood and thick bark made excellent firewood. The wood's strength and durability favored it for spears and harpoon shafts, even fish-hooks. The pitch was used as a salve and also in caulking canoes.

The Douglas-fir has been embraced for plantation forestry by several countries in Western Europe—especially in France and Germany, where there are now several million of these trees.

'PITCHFORK' BRACTS

COASTAL FORM   INTERIOR FORM

Range: Wide range and from low to middle elevations. East of the Cascades it has a shorter, more rugged form.

Before Douglas knew that the Douglas-fir would be named after him, he described it as follows: 'Tree remarkably tall, unusually straight, having the pyramid form— one of the truly graceful objects in Nature.'

WESTERN HEMLOCK
Tsuga heterophylla

A quick distinguishing feature is the **drooping tip**, most clearly seen on a younger tree. **Needles, whitish beneath because of 2 thin lines of stomata, are of unequal length**—about 1.3 cm (1/2")—and roughly 2-ranked. Cone length is about 2.5 cm (1"), half that of mountain hemlock.

This tree was recognized as a new species by Lewis and Clark, probably in 1805. It was all around Fort Clatsop, and they mention it in general terms on February 5, 1805. For many decades it was so overshadowed by the giants of the forest—Douglas-fir, western redcedar and Sitka spruce—that it was classed as a weed tree. It was and remains the most continuously distributed and **most common tree of the great coniferous rainforest**. Hemlocks have been measured to 2.4 m (8') in diameter and 60 m (200') tall, but in mature forests most measure around 1.2 m (4') in diameter. The shade beneath these trees is so dense that other species are unable to grow, so hemlock tends to create a forest with a single tree species. You can often see where hemlock seeds have fallen on an old rotting log (a 'nurse log') and sprouted a line of trees that will eventually straddle the log with large roots.

By the 1930s, western hemlock was being recognized for its true value—as a source of good lumber for certain types of construction, as an excellent pulp tree and as wildlife habitat.

Native American groups used it extensively. Tannin in the bark was used in tanning hides, and the inner bark was eaten. The easily worked wood was shaped into a variety of implements.

Range: A tree of low to middle elevations, it ranges to 900 m (3000') in elevation. Mostly confined to the western slopes of the Cascades. Very limited in the interior cedar-hemlock ecosystem. (See map, p. 21.)

MOUNTAIN HEMLOCK

Tsuga mertensiana

Has the same characteristic **drooping tip** as western hemlock, but **needles are equal in length**. Note that the needles may tend to bush around the twigs rather than the 2-ranked appearance of western hemlock. At 2.5–5 cm (1–2''), **cones are twice as long as on western hemlock. Trunks and limbs are usually twisted and contorted** and at high elevations the tree is much dwarfed.

Range: At elevations of **900–2150 m (3000–7000'),** *above the range of western hemlock.* **Typically, in the subalpine and found with subalpine fir and yellow-cedar. Western slopes of coastal mountain ranges and Cascades.**

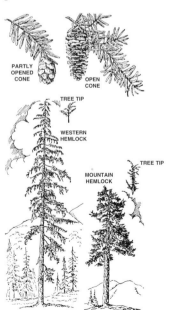

PARTLY OPENED CONE

OPEN CONE

TREE TIP

WESTERN HEMLOCK

TREE TIP

MOUNTAIN HEMLOCK

VANCOUVER   BRITISH COLUMBIA

VAN. ISLAND

Bellingham   Republic

VICTORIA

EVERETT

Grand Coulee

SEATTLE   WENATCHEE   SPOKANE

TACOMA   Cle Elum

IDAHO

YAKIMA

Goldendale

PORTLAND   COLUMBIA   RIVER

OREGON

WESTERN HEMLOCK

MOUNTAIN HEMLOCK

WESTERN REDCEDAR
Thuja plicata

A **giant among the conifers** of the world and the provincial tree of neighboring British Columbia. Redcedars are known to have reached 6 m (20') in diameter, 60 m (200') in height and at least 1500 years of age. Today, many remaining trees are over 45 m (145') tall and 2 m (6 1/2') in diameter. Massive, fluted trunks, often hollow, culminate in a **spike-like dead top. Frond-like branches** are a distinctive yellowish-green color. Small, woody seed cones.

Archibald Menzies, on Captain George Vancouver's expedition in the early 1790s, must have seen western redcedar almost immediately, but his naming of it was in 1824.

In 1900 Captain J.C. Voss bought an 11.6 m (38') redcedar dugout. He added a cabin and 3 masts and sailed around the world. This boat stands complete today in the Maritime Museum of British Columbia in Victoria. Redcedar is prized for its close-grained texture and satiny smooth finish. A **natural oil makes the wood quite immune to decay** and so it is used for boats, water tanks and tubs, greenhouses and posts. Redcedar wood is popular in the U.S. and Canada for making shakes, shingles and siding for buildings.

To the coastal aboriginal peoples, this species was truly the 'Tree of Life.' In its range from Alaska to California, it was the plant most widely used by Native Americans. They found the bark soft and pliable enough to make clothes, baskets and mats. The easily split wood produced canoes as well as immense beams for house construction. Intricately carved totem poles and masks of redcedar are testimony to the level of cultural development of these people.

Range: Best growth and abundance in *wet soils west of the Cascades* and below 1050 m (3500'). East of the Cascades it fringes some streams and wet places, reaching to 1500 m (5000') elevation. Roadside streams in Mt. Spokane Park.

In June 1805, Lewis and Clark came to the westward slope of the Rocky Mountains. Later, they searched for trees suitable for making boats. They were in present-day northern Idaho before they saw an 'Arbor-vitae that is very common and grows to a great size being from 2–6' in diameter.' With crude tools they made themselves 4 large boats and a smaller boat to scout ahead. Thus the last phase of their long trip to the Pacific Ocean was made possible by the fine natural qualities of the redcedar.

Clark, November 1805, 'The women wore a short petticoat of the inner bark of the white cedar or arber vita which hang down loose in strings nearly as low as the knee....'

YELLOW-CEDAR
Chamaecyparis nootkatensis

The *nootka* part of the botanical name refers to a remote area on the west coast of Vancouver Island, B.C. Although Archibald Menzies had recorded yellow-cedar in the early 1790s, it wasn't until 1824 that it had an approved scientific name.

Note a **drooping leader**, like western hemlock, **branchlets hanging almost vertically**, and a **tree often warped and twisted**. There is nothing to confuse it with at higher elevations.

Because of severe climatic conditions, yellow-cedar grows slowly. In some special habitats this tree has grown to giant size and age and, at 1800 years and older, some specimens could have rated as the oldest living things in nearby British Columbia, where it is more abundant and grows larger.

If there still is doubt about identification, try a branch-needle test. Rub your fingers **against the grain of a twig—yellow-cedar is prickly** because the scaly leaves are sharp-pointed and spreading, but western redcedar feels smooth. If you have a chance to see it, the **raw wood has a distinct yellow color and a smell all its own**. The wood is straight-grained, uniform and 'cuts and carves like butter,' says a wood-carving friend. No wonder it is a favorite with carvers. Boat-builders use it because it resists rot. It has limited commercial value because of its restricted range and relative scarcity, but remains much sought-after.

Native American groups prized yellow-cedar wood for making bows, paddles and small utensils. Like almost every plant whose wood the aboriginal peoples used, its cones, bark and twigs were thought to have special medicinal qualities.

Range: In general, this tree is at *higher elevations than western redcedar.* Coastal mountain elevations for it range from 900 m (3000') to timberline. Along the Hurricane Ridge road in the Olympics and both mountain roads on Mt. Rainier, cedars over the elevation of 1050 m (3500') will be yellow-cedar. Eastern slope of Chinook Pass (just east of Mt. Rainier National Park). Higher elevations of the North Cascades Highway (State Route 20).

David Douglas, upon reaching the Columbia River after a long ocean voyage from England, made his headquarters at Fort Vancouver, which had been just recently constructed. Douglas, April 16, 1825, 'The chief factor John McLoughlin Esq. ...received me with much kindness. I showed him my instructions...and talked over my pursuit in the most frank and handsome manner. He assured me that everything in his power would be done....' Douglas was to meet him later in the wilderness. 'He was such a figure as I should not like to meet on a dark night...dressed in clothes that had once been fashionable but now covered with a thousand patches of different colors...loaded with arms...his own herculean dimensions...that would convey a good idea of the highway men of former days.'

SITKA SPRUCE
Picea sitchensis

If close to the ocean, Sitka spruce is distinctive, with huge, out-thrust branches from which branchlets droop. If slightly more inland and part of a forest with western redcedar, Douglas-fir and hemlock, then it can be a tall, conical tree with a thick, straight trunk. Check by feeling a branchlet—the stiff, sharp needles of a Sitka spruce will make it feel prickly all around. Under the tree there are usually cones. They are scaly, light brown, cylindrical and 5–7.5 cm (2–3") long.

David Douglas introduced this tree by seed, along with many others, to Britain and today it is the most popular tree for reforestation. Sitka spruce has the **highest strength-to-weight ratio** of all forest trees. Its straight-grained timber, which doesn't warp or split, was in great demand during World War II.

The HK-1, or 'Spruce Goose,' was an experimental flying boat of tremendous size. It was designed by multimillionaire Howard Hughes as a way of transporting 600–700 soldiers per trip across the Atlantic during World War II, when German submarines were taking a terrific toll on shipping. Because only non-strategic materials could be used, the

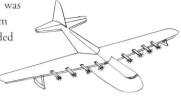

giant plane was made of wood. The plane was 67.1 m (220') long, with a wingspan of 97.5 m (320'). Eight 3000 horsepower engines provided the power.

Sitka spruce was ideal for the plane's main framing, and most of it came from the Pacific Northwest. Birch and poplar from the East were used for plywood to make the covering. With Hughes at the controls on November 2, 1947, it lifted off the water and flew for nearly 1.6 km (1 mile)—the only flight it ever made! Problems arose, the project was dropped. Today the Spruce Goose, in excellent condition, is on display at the Michael King Smith Evergreen Aviation Educational Center, near McMinnville, Oregon.

Spruce is also used for shipbuilding, plywood, pulp and soundboards for musical instruments. It is easily glued and painted. It was highly valued by aboriginal peoples. The inner bark was either eaten raw or dried into cakes. The pitch had many reputed medicinal qualities, for ailments such as skin irritations and rheumatism. An unusual use of this spruce was watertight baskets and hats made from small spruce roots split into very thin strings and interwoven with other materials.

Range: A tree of the coastal region from Alaska southward through B.C. into the Puget Sound area. Also in the Olympics, especially in the Hoh Valley, where it reaches giant size. Its range coincides with the rainiest parts of North America and extends up major river valleys for 80 km (50 miles) and more inland, at elevations up to 600 m (2000').

Lewis, February 4, 1806, 'A species which grows to an immense size very commonly 20 feet in girth six feet above...the earth. The timber is white and soft and rives [splits] better than any other species.'

Douglas, 1828 or 1829, 'It possesses one great advantage by growing to a very large size on Northern declivities...in apparently poor, thin, damp soils....It could thrive in such places in Britain.'

27

ENGELMANN SPRUCE
Picea engelmannii

Travelers in the Pacific Northwest entranced by the scenic aspect of mountain streams and lakes and the sweep of high mountains probably don't know that Engelmann spruce is responsible for a great share of that beauty. However, this tree is **frequently the major evergreen component in the high mountains** and is often featured in sketches and paintings. The conical stateliness and dark green foliage alone may provide sufficient

interest for some, but to tie a name to the tree that you are seeing, note that spruce **needles are 4-sided, not flat like on most other conifers**. The needles can be rolled between the fingers and, if one is pulled off, it should leave a small spur on the twig. This spur is only fly-speck sized and it is better to look along the twig for old spurs. The **only other native spruce in Washington is Sitka spruce,** p. 26, and its range is different, so identification is simplified.

This tree is most abundant between 900 m (3000') and 2150 m (7000') elevation on moist mountain slopes. Because **seedlings can establish in heavy shade**, Engelmann spruce often forms a large, spreading thicket. If you are a hiker, you may have been grateful to dive into such cover when a mountain storm developed suddenly.

At and near timberline, this spruce mingles with subalpine fir. With a narrow crown, Engelmann spruce's shape isn't as sharp-pointed as with subalpine fir and its **small, tassel-like branchlets hang down**. If you see small cones under a tree in this ecosystem, it is likely an Engelmann spruce, but note that mountain hemlock, p. 21, in the same elevation range, also produces cones.

Range: Found high on westerly slopes of the Cascades, but more common on easterly slopes from 1200 m (4000') to near timberline, where it mingles with subalpine fir. Pend Oreille and Ferry counties, Blue Mountains and Olympics.

Despite the rigors of a day's travel, which usually started at dawn and often went to dusk, Douglas managed to keep detailed notes. It wasn't unusual for him to estimate that he had 'gained' about 65 km (40 miles) a day. And imagine the number of stops he

made to examine some aspect or other of natural history. His daily notes about weather conditions make you realize that fall, winter and early spring each produced its full share of miserable trail conditions.

Douglas, October 25, 1825, 'The rain driven by the violence of the wind, rendered it impossible for me to keep any fire, and to add misery to my affliction my tent was blown down at midnight, when I lay among bracken rolled in my wet blanket....'

WESTERN YEW
Taxus brevifolia

This tree can easily go unnoticed. If you could attribute shyness to a tree, it could best fit western yew. Is it purposely hiding its untidy, mis-shapen form under other trees? Once you become familiar with the **ungainly limb structure** and the **dull green color of the needles**, then it becomes recognized as quite widespread. Most yew trees won't be larger than 30 cm (12") in diameter and 6 m (20') tall. There are exceptions and under favorable conditions these measurements can double (or more).

Check to see that the **needles are flat and sharp-pointed, have short stems, are roughly 2-ranked** (rather like western hemlock) and measure 1.3–2 cm (1/2–3/4") long. You might have to search to find the tell-tale fruits, for they grow only on the female trees, which appear to be few compared to the males. They are **rounded seeds partly enclosed by a scarlet, fleshy and open-ended button** and are best seen from late summer into autumn. Not edible to humans but favored by birds, who disperse them.

The medicinal qualities of the bark received worldwide attention when it was discovered that a chemical in the bark, taxol, was proving effective against certain types of cancer. One treatment requires 2 g (0.07 oz) of taxol, which would come from 10 good-sized trees.

Yew species provided fighting bows for ancient armies and are valued today for the same purpose by do-it-yourself archers.

The contrast between yellow sapwood and rich, red heartwood makes this yew desirable for carving and small, ornamental woodwork. When coastal Native Americans set out to capture a huge gray whale, a chief of high stature was the one to throw the harpoon. The shaft of the harpoon was yew wood. Coastal aboriginal peoples used the yew for a wide variety of implements, wherever strength, toughness and durability were required. It was prized in the making of bows and yet Clark, in the note below, gives quite a different description of the bows that he saw.

Range: This small understory tree, usually mixed with other conifers, prefers moist areas, streamsides and canyons, but also occurs on dry hillsides. Northwestern region of the state, from sea level to 1500 m (5000'). Olympics and Cascades, but favoring western slopes.

Clark, January 15, 1806, 'Their bows are extremely neat and very elastic...they are very flat and thin, formed of the heart of the arbor-vita [western redcedar] or white cedar, the back of the bow being thickly covered with sinews of the Elk laid on with a Gleue which they made from sturgeon.'

NOBLE FIR

Abies procera

True firs (*Abies* spp.) have many features different from other conifers. When a needle is removed, it leaves a very small, circular scar. This feature is best seen by looking on a twig for old scars rather than making a new one. Identify the symmetrical noble fir by needles that twist upward. These **needles are somewhat 4-sided, with a silvery sheen that results from 2 distinct white rows of stomata beneath; the upper surface is grooved**, with 1–2 whitish rows of stomata. Cones, if you can see them near the top, are erect and 10–15 cm (4–6″) long. They disintegrate rather than fall. Noble fir is rated highly for timber quality and was used in airplane construction during World War II.

Range: This tree of *middle mountain elevations*, **600–1500 m (2000–5000'), usually grows with Douglas-fir and western hemlock. Found on both sides of the Cascade Mountains. Stevens Pass southward to Crater Falls. On Mt. Rainier from middle to upper elevations.**

David Douglas found this tree in 1830 while exploring mountain slopes in the southern Cascades. He called it Abies nobilis, *but the botanical name was changed when that one was found to be already in use.*

Douglas, 1830, 'I spent 3 weeks in a forest composed of this tree, and day by day could not cease to admire it....' He collected seed and sent it to England, the start of plantations that are highly prized today.

GRAND FIR
Abies grandis

The **most common of the true firs** (*Abies* spp.) in Washington. Identify by **needles in 2 flattened rows, dark yellowish-green and grooved, 2 white lines beneath**. Note a sweet balsam odor— a cherished part of the Christmas scene. From a distance the rounded, thick-limbed top of the tree is fair identification. Cones are erect, 10–15 cm (4–6") long and disintegrate on the tree. Most mature trees average 60–90 cm (2–3') in diameter and to 41 m (135') tall. An unusual feature of this tree is that it can grow limbs on a trunk that once was bare because of heavy shade.

Range: Occurs with Douglas-fir, western hemlock and western redcedar. Grows best in valley bottoms but is found at up to 1500 m (5000') elevation. Coast forest and mountain forest ecosystems, both west and east of the Cascades; especially in valleys that drain into Puget Sound.

*Douglas, April 30, 1826, 'On arriving at camp one gathers a few dried twigs and makes fire, two or three procuring fuel for the night, and as many more gathering soft branches of **Abies** or **Tsuga** to sleep on, termed "flooring the house," each hanging his wet clothes by the fire, repairing snowshoes, and arranging his load for the ensuing day....'*

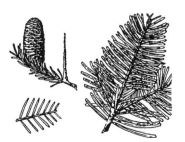

AMABILIS FIR
Abies amabilis

When open-grown, these **trees are unusually symmetrical and spire-pointed, with lower branches sweeping downward** to near the ground. Many trees are 80 cm (2 1/2') in diameter and 30 m (100') tall. Despite its size and form, this fir tends to lose its distinctiveness in a forest of Douglas-fir, western hemlock, western redcedar and Sitka spruce. At high elevations it **resembles subalpine fir**.

For identification, note that the **needles twist upward to produce a flattish effect** when seen from beneath. **Needles on the top of a twig point forward**. The needles are flat and most are notched, a bright green above and 2 to several white lines (rows of stomata) beneath. The difficult-to-see **purple cones are upright** and measure 9–15 cm (3 1/2–6'') in length. They disintegrate rather than fall. The bark contains resin-filled blisters.

Also known as: Pacific silver fir, balsam fir.
Range: From sea level to 1850 m (6000'). Olympics and both slopes of the Cascades.

Douglas, in 1825, found this beautiful tree not far from Mt. St. Helens. He named it amabilis, or 'lovely.' He wrote, 'This is another tree of singular beauty...the branches are very long, drooping and flat.' He collected seeds for horticultural use in Britain and so this tree became known to Europe.

SUBALPINE FIR
Abies lasiocarpa

Confused by all the needle shapes and designs of the true firs? What makes subalpine fir distinctive? The **bluish-green needles turn upward** in brush-like fashion and **both surfaces of needles have white lines** (rows of stomata) on them. Stomata allow leaves to take in carbon dioxide (for photosynthesis) and to give off oxygen.

If you are enjoying picturesque trees in subalpine terrain, chances are that they are subalpine fir. Also compare to amabilis fir and Engelmann spruce. From a large tree to 30 m (100') tall at lower elevations of around 600 m (2000'), it decreases in size with increasing elevation, becoming dwarfed at timberline. Sometimes it forms a dense thicket with long boughs spreading along the ground. The pyramidal shape, with stiff, down-sloping branches, is adapted for winter storms. Cones are a dark purple and break apart on the tree, leaving an erect spike. Once called alpine fir, the name was changed to subalpine fir to conform with the concept that trees don't grow in alpine terrain.

Also known as: alpine fir.

Range: Occurs on all the *higher mountain systems* of Washington. See it at the roadside in high mountain passes. A feature of the scenery in high national parks.

Archibald Menzies, exploring the Puget Sound area in 1792, went ashore to find '...a fine level Country...covered with pine forests...abounding with clear spots....A Traveller wandering over these unfrequented Plains is regaled with a salubrious & vivifying air impregnated with the Balsamic fragrance of the surrounding Pinery.'

PONDEROSA PINE

Pinus ponderosa

'Of all the Pines this one gives forth the finest music to the winds,' wrote **John Muir**. At the tender age of 10, I hadn't heard of John Muir, but I did know there was something very magical about climbing to the top of a ponderosa pine and enjoying the whisper of the wind through the needles.

This distinctive tree has a straight trunk and a loose mass of heavy branches. Especially on older trees, the **bark is an attractive terra-cotta red**, marked by lengthwise furrows that resemble jig-saw pieces. The **3 long needles to a sheath** and the large cones are distinctive features. Although John Muir measured a ponderosa pine in the Sierras that was 2.4 m (8') in diameter and 67 m (220') tall, few trees even as much as 1 m (3 1/2') in diameter are seen now.

Ponderosa pine grows over 260 million ha (1 million sq. mi.) of this continent and is judged by some to be the greatest among all the pines in North America. It ranks close to Douglas-fir as a timber-producing tree. There is a flammable chemical in the needles that produces a quick and very hot ground fire when the fallen needles burn. A ground fire of this kind doesn't damage the thick-barked tree but does destroy competing vegetation.

Although the Lewis and Clark Expedition collected this pine in 1805, a series of misadventures kept it from being officially recognized and named. David Douglas recognized it as a new species in 1826 and later named it 'ponderosa.' To the north, famed explorers of Canada—such as Sir Alexander Mackenzie, Simon Fraser and David Thompson—crossed immense tracts of wilderness where these trees grew but, without any botanical training, they were unable to classify or scientifically name any plants. Although these 3 explorers didn't achieve botanical fame, they are remembered in the naming of 3 mighty Canadian rivers.

Aboriginal peoples used the bark scales to make a quick, smokeless fire that gave no clue to their presence. The cambium layer from young trees was collected and eaten, as were the seeds.

Also known as: yellow pine.

Range: A common tree of lower forests in central and eastern Washington. Usually found at 450–1050 m (1500–3500') elevation. Okanogan, Chelan, Yakima, Klickitat, Spokane counties and eastern half of the Columbia Gorge. Small pockets in central Washington. Scattered groves or patches here and there in lowlands west of the Cascades and south of Tacoma.

Lewis, May 8, 1806, '...I observed many pine trees which appear to have been cut down...in order to collect the seed of the long leaf pine which in those moments of distress also furnishes an article of food; the seed....is about the size...of the large sunflower, they are not unpleasant when roasted or boiled, during this month the natives also peel this pine and eat the succulent or inner bark.'

WESTERN WHITE PINE
Pinus monticola

Although David Douglas mentioned very large trees in his journals, today a big western white pine would be 90 cm (3') in diameter and 37 m (120') tall. The Latin *monticola* means 'inhabiting mountains.' Indeed, a handsome tree, with a **remarkable symmetry of shape** and **limbs in whorls**, best seen in young trees. And again a tree easy to identify, for it is the **only 5-needle pine below subalpine elevations**. Needles are 5–13 cm (2–5") long, about twice the length of those on whitebark pine. They drop in quantity and persist on the ground, giving the hiker a good clue to the tree's presence. Also note the **long cones, 10–25 cm (4–10") in length**.

The great forests of white pine were largely decimated by white pine blister rust soon after the disease was introduced from France in 1910. You will still notice trees dying from it today. The disease needs currants or gooseberries as alternate hosts to complete its life cycle.

The wood is fine grained and usually free from defects, so it is an ideal wood for carving and special construction purposes. Loggers value it more than Douglas-fir or western redcedar. Beginning in 1914, it was for many years the ideal wood for matches. A tea from the bark and preparations from the pitch had various medicinal uses among Native American peoples.

OPEN

CLOSED

Range: Generally at middle elevations, but reaching to subalpine at times. Characteristically found in the mountain forest ecosystem of the Olympics, Cascades and mountains of northeastern Washington. Higher elevations of the North Cascades Highway (State Route 20).

David Douglas was on the slopes of Mt. St. Helens when he identified this tree in 1832. He wrote, 'A handsome tree of large dimensions...in the mountain valleys...also in rocky, bare, thin soils it particularly abounds. They naturally prune themselves leaving a clean trunk.'

WHITEBARK PINE
Pinus albicaulis

Another pine that poses no identi-fication problems. Whitebark pine is the **only pine that you will find at elevations of 1500 m (5000') and above**. Usually a sturdy, twisted tree with several trunks, it can be a misshapen shrub at timberline. Notice the **white bark on younger limbs**, the 5 needles per sheath and the heavy cones that hang downward. Clark's nutcracker, a bird of the mountains, pries them apart for the large seeds.

Range: High elevations in the Cascades and Olympics. See it near and above both lodges on Mt. Rainier, high on Mt. Baker and growing along higher sections of the Pacific Crest National Scenic Trail in the North Cascades.

LODGEPOLE PINE
Pinus contorta var. latifolia

Although lodgepole pine is often called jack pine, this reference more properly applies to *P. banksiana*, a close relative found east of the Rockies. Lodgepole pine is a **2-needle pine**—the only other one native to Washington is shore pine, p. 41. Because it grows with other conifers, it can go unnoticed. However, once you learn to recognize this tall, slender tree, rarely more than 35 cm (14") in diameter and 30 m (100') tall, with regular whorls of bushy, up-pointing limbs, you will see it many places.

East of the Cascades, it is usually in pure stands that look as if they were intentionally planted that way. This effect occurs because of the way forest fires heat and open the resin-filled cones, freeing the seeds. For many years this tree had little use except for fuel, railroad ties and mine timbers. Now it is important for small-dimension lumber.

Also known as: jack pine.

Range: Most abundant east of the Cascades, particularly in Ferry and Pend Oreille counties. Although only in scattered patches to the west of the Cascades, this pine is widely distributed. Grows sparsely almost anywhere in the coast forest ecosystem, but favors the San Juan Islands and Puget Sound.

SHORE PINE
Pinus contorta var. contorta

A coastal version of lodgepole pine, p. 40. It can take on truly contorted shapes, a feature that David Douglas noted when he gave it its Latin name. This picturesque form was used to advantage in landscaping some coastal properties—note its use in the Long Beach area, where it also grows wild.

Range: Boggy areas along the coast in sandy or dry, gravelly soils. More abundant a few kilometers inland.

Clark, December 8, 1805, '...I sunk into the mud and water up to my hips...small knobs are promisquisly scattered about which are steep and thickly covered with pine Common to the Country....' Likely he was in the Long Beach area.

Douglas, 1828 or 1829, 'Branches drooping, greatly twisted in every direction. Little can be said in favour of this tree either for ornament or as a useful wood.'

Douglas, March 25, 1826 (elsewhere in the state), '...at daylight we resumed our route, sleet and with a keen north wind. Being almost benumbed with cold, I preferred walking along the bank of the river although my path in many places was very rugged.'

ROCKY MOUNTAIN JUNIPER

Juniperus scopulorum

Both Rocky Mountain juniper and western juniper can, under severe conditions of habitat, be more like shrubs than trees. However, Rocky Mountain juniper is commonly 1.8–6 m (6–20') tall and has trunks up to 30 cm (12") in diameter. Several thick trunks may occur and create a massive, bushy effect. Identification is often confused because there usually are **2 different kinds of leaves**: young shoots with sharp, needle-like leaves and older branches with smooth, scaly ones like a cedar. To definitely distinguish from western juniper, p. 43, note that the back of each **scale-like leaf of Rocky Mountain juniper has no gland** (seen as a minute depression on a leaf of the other juniper).

Fleshy, berry-like cones are lumpy and bluish-purple. They take 2 years to fully ripen. Juniper seed is difficult to germinate because of its tough, fleshy covering. However, birds and animals that eat these seeds do the job by passing them through their digestive tracts.

In the days when the pencil was the main writing implement, a closely related eastern juniper provided the wood for most pencils, but substituting this western juniper never proved as successful. And, although this tree has a contrasting white sapwood and red heartwood, the wood is too soft for the best of carving and ornamental work.

Note: A low, sprawling juniper classed as a shrub is on p. 125.

Range: Never common, it is found on dry, rocky terrain of the San Juan Islands and bordering Puget Sound and high northern ridges of the Olympics. Fairly abundant on mountain slopes above the eastern end of the Columbia Gorge. Sporadic in drylands of southeastern Washington.

Archibald Menzies, June 17, 1792, reported that, after landing on an island in Puget Sound where '...the shores were rocky, rugged & cliffs rising into the hills...we found growing some trees of Red Cedar [actually Rocky Mountain juniper].'

WESTERN JUNIPER
Juniperus occidentalis

Very similar to Rocky Mountain juniper, p. 42, in varying from shrub-like to tree-like. In general, **a juniper of great size** will be this one. Specimens near Sunnyside and Bickelton are up to 45 cm (18") in diameter and 9 m (30') tall. Trunks often branch into sturdy limbs. The stringy bark is often furrowed with brown-cinnamon tones. **On the back of each scale-like leaf there is a gland** (minute shallow pit)—perhaps the best and quickest way to tell it from Rocky Mountain juniper, which lacks this feature.

Range: Dry foothills and low mountains from Yakima County southward. Klickitat and Asotin counties.

43

WESTERN LARCH
Larix occidentalis

Identification is easy and positive if you can see the **needle clusters arising from knobs on the twigs**. There are 1–2 dozen 2.5 cm (1") long needles in a cluster. An attractive light green color, the **needles turn golden in late September and then fall**. In winter and early spring, note a straight tapering trunk perhaps to 1.2 m (4') thick and 45 m (150') tall—a large tree today, but they do grow larger. **Bark on mature trees is furrowed, scaly and orange-red**, a little deeper in color than ponderosa pine. The thick bark makes it fire resistant. Trees have an open crown and you can distinctly see the **short, horizontal branches with an up-curve to their tips**. When the needles have fallen, the trees look dead.

The wood from this fast-growing larch is very durable, even when in contact with the ground, and is favored for greenhouse lumber, mine timbers, fence posts and special construction needs. Commercially, it is considered an important tree.

Note: Larches resemble evergreens during spring and summer, but the needles turn yellow and fall in autumn.

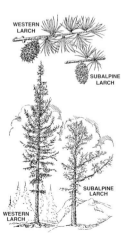

Range: Generally east of the Cascades, but turns up here and there over a wide range of mountain forests. Elevation limits are 800 m (2600') and 1500 m (5000'). You may find 1–2 trees or a pocket of them or a belt among other conifers. Most common in the northeastern areas of the state. Also in the Blue Mountains. Its location is easily noted and beautifully marked when it is in fall color. (See map, p. 45.)

SUBALPINE LARCH

Larix lyalli

D r. David Lyall, a surgeon and a botanist too, was part of the survey crew of 1858–60 that had been sent to mark the 49th parallel as the boundary between Canada and the United States. Likely he sighted subalpine larch near the northern boundary of the Pasayten Wilderness Area in Washington, which displays a fine growth of these trees. The form varies from a fairly upright but limby tree to a crooked, twisted and dwarfed shape near timberline—a photographer's delight, especially when the needles are pure gold in color. This species differs from western larch, p. 44, in having **hairy twigs and needles 4-sided in cross section** rather than flat.

Range: Easterly slopes of the Cascades at subalpine elevations from B.C. south to the Wenatchee Mountains. Harts Pass (on border between Whatcom and Okanogan counties).

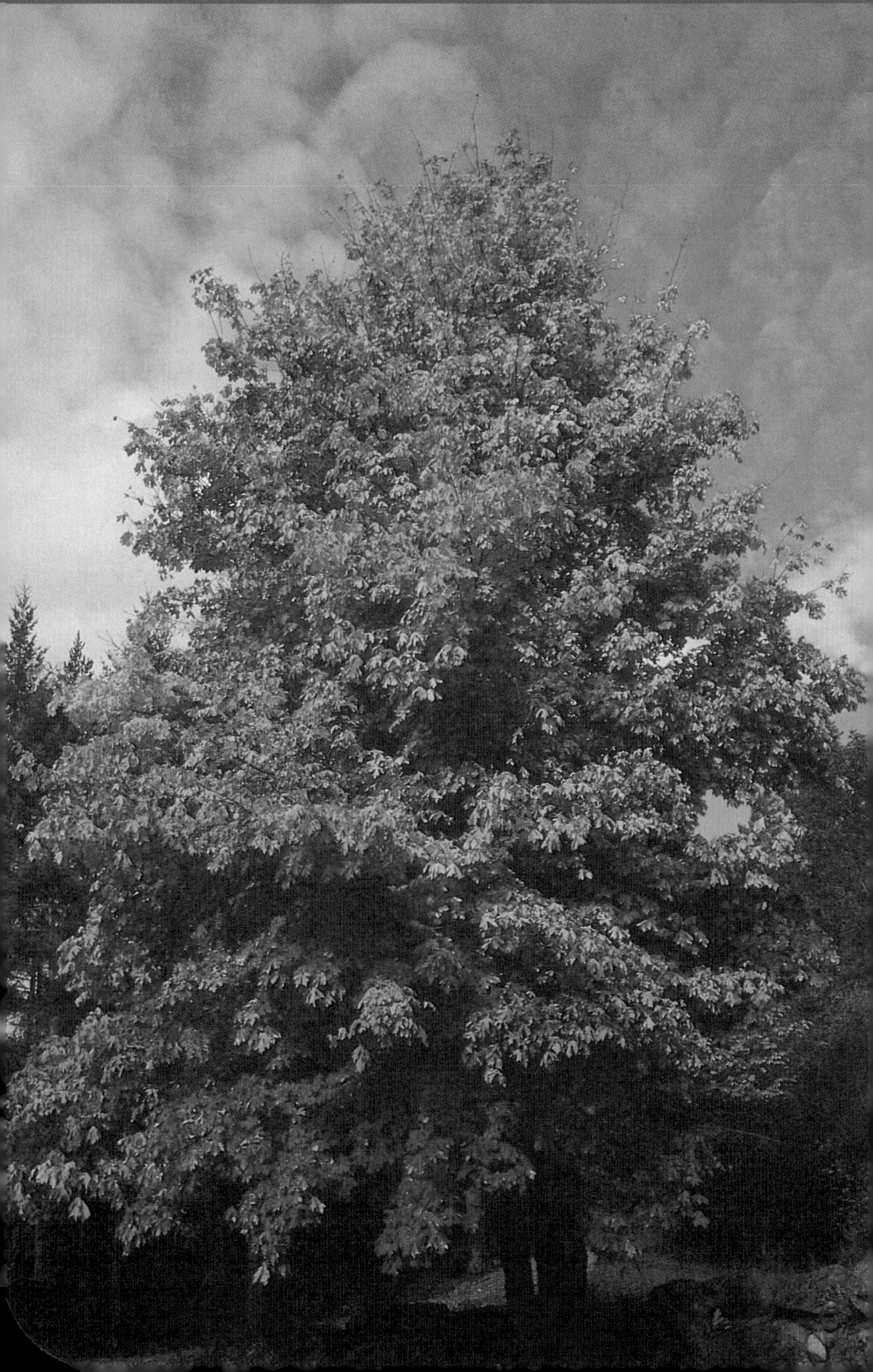

KEY TO BROADLEAF TREES

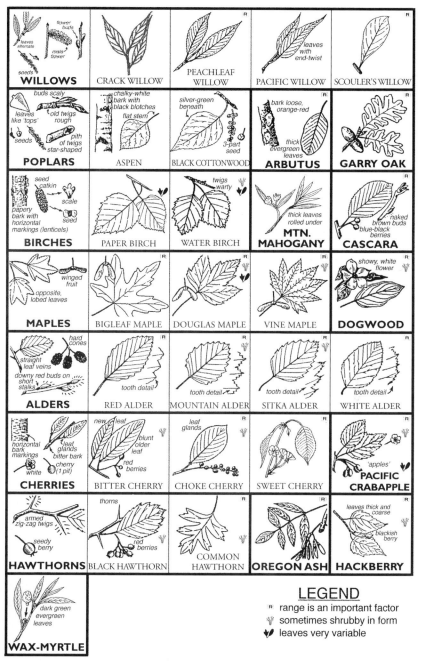

WILLOWS	CRACK WILLOW	PEACHLEAF WILLOW	PACIFIC WILLOW	SCOULER'S WILLOW
POPLARS	ASPEN	BLACK COTTONWOOD	**ARBUTUS**	**GARRY OAK**
BIRCHES	PAPER BIRCH	WATER BIRCH	**MTN. MAHOGANY**	**CASCARA**
MAPLES	BIGLEAF MAPLE	DOUGLAS MAPLE	VINE MAPLE	**DOGWOOD**
ALDERS	RED ALDER	MOUNTAIN ALDER	SITKA ALDER	WHITE ALDER
CHERRIES	BITTER CHERRY	CHOKE CHERRY	SWEET CHERRY	**PACIFIC CRABAPPLE**
HAWTHORNS	BLACK HAWTHORN	COMMON HAWTHORN	**OREGON ASH**	**HACKBERRY**
WAX-MYRTLE				

LEGEND

ᴿ range is an important factor
🌱 sometimes shrubby in form
🍃 leaves very variable

ARBUTUS
Arbutus menziesii

A tree so distinctive that it immediately catches your eye and your interest. Its **picturesque, twisting trunk** is a unique **orange-red color** and, except for large areas of exfoliating (shedding) bark, mostly exhibits a polished smoothness. In spring the arbutus is decorated with **clusters of white flowers** that become red berries during fall and winter. **Leaves are evergreen, thick and leathery**. During their second year, many leaves turn red and drop; they are rather slow to decay.

Named in 1814 in honor of the pioneer botanist Archibald Menzies, who recorded it when he came ashore in 1792 at Port Discovery. Another name, madrone, is common here and to the south of us. It arose when a Spanish priest noted in 1769 that there were many *madronos*. He was likening this tree to the related *madrono* or strawberry tree of the Mediterranean.

It is unfortunate that such a crop of

large, red berries, which ripen in fall and persist into winter, could not have been an important food source for aboriginal peoples. In fact, they were unpalatable enough to be avoided, although there were some medicinal properties attributed to the bark and leaves. Nevertheless, the berries are a valuable food source to robins, varied thrushes and band-tailed pigeons.

The wood, with its outward promise of something very desirable, fails to be so. Although workable when green, it dries to become a hard, brittle wood of little commercial value.

Note: Arbutus's 'evergreen' leaves are only partially deciduous.

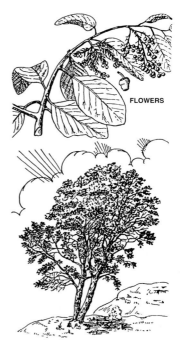

FLOWERS

Also known as: Madrone.

Range: 'If there are arbutus, can rock be far beneath?' is applicable, for arbutus favors open, sunny places along rock bluffs and canyons. Generally not too far from the ocean, as if it enjoyed an ocean view, it is commonly associated with Garry oak and stunted Douglas-fir. San Juan Islands, dry rocky places around the shore of Puget Sound, but not along the exposed outer coast. From easterly lowlands of the Olympics to southern Washington.

Clark, November 30, 1805, 'I walked on the point [bank of lower Columbia River] and observed rose bushes, different Species of pine, a Spe[c]ies of ash, alder, a Species of wild Crab loral [arbutus]....'

Lewis, December 1, 1805, '...the tree bears a red berry in clusters of a round form...the leaf like that of a small magnolia, and bark smooth and of a brick dust red colour it appears to be of the evergreen kind.'

Douglas collected seeds in 'mountainous woody parts of N.W. Coast of North America,' and horticultural specimens were grown in England soon afterward.

GARRY OAK

Quercus garryana

The **only native oak** in Washington, it ranges widely, from oceanside to interior mountains. So typical are its form, **lobed oak leaves and acorns** that it stands in a category by itself. **Leaves are thick and leathery**, a moisture-preservation adaptation.

Usually a massive tree with thick, gnarled limbs and huge shaggy crown. In rocky, exposed places, Garry oak may form a thicket of small, twisted trees. Fine specimens growing in parklands of wildflowers consistently measure to 90 cm (3') in diameter and up to 35 m (115') tall. They often live for 500 years.

Although the attractive acorns are much favored by gray squirrels, band-tailed pigeons and Steller's jays, they weren't easily prepared as food by Native Americans because of the bitter tannin content.

Range: From the San Juan Islands southward here and there through Puget Sound to the Columbia River and eastward to The Dalles. From there, northward to Goldendale and Toppenish. An impressive grove at Fort Simcoe.

Clark, October 26, 1805, '...our hunters saw elk and bear signs today in the white oake woods....Country thinly timbered with pine [ponderosa] and white oak [Garry]. Our men danced tonight—dried all our wet articles and repaired our canoes.'

Clark, November 1, 1805, '...we got from these people a fiew pounded roos [roots] fish and Acorns of white oake, these Acorns they make use of as food raw & roasted....'

This oak was among the many trees that David Douglas found and named in the lower valley of the Columbia River. He noted that the oaks were '...generally low and scrubby and interspersed over the country in an open manner....' As for the name, Douglas wrote, 'I have great pleasure in dedicating this species to N. Garry Esq; Deputy Governor of the Hudson's Bay Company.'

Douglas, 1825, 'By several of the native tribes they [the acorns] are gathered in the months of August and September, and deposited in pits [near water] so that they are completely covered by water, in which they lie till the following winter, when they are taken out and without any preparation...are eaten as an article of food.'

WESTERN FLOWERING DOGWOOD

Cornus nuttallii

The western flowering dogwood, a small tree to 20 m (65') tall, could be easily overlooked for much of the year among the rich growth of the Pacific Coast. However, at the **peak of its bloom in May**, during a **possible second flowering in September**, and later, with its **clumps of bright red berries**, it is worthy of high honor. The inflorescence (bloom) is 5–13 cm (2–5") across, with 4–6 showy white bracts that surround a rounded **knob of small, greenish flowers** that later turn into red berries. Leaves are opposite, 7.5–10 cm (3–4") long. Veins curve parallel to leaf edges.

The unusual name of dogwood might have arisen from the wood being used as skewers or 'dags.' Now this hard, heavy wood is favored for such items as spindles and piano keys.

Range: Most common at up to 450 m (1500') elevation on the western slopes of the Cascades. Range extends eastward along Columbia Gorge as far as Bingen and from there northward in the mountain forest ecosystem.

The nuttallii part of the scientific name has a most interesting origin. Although David Douglas was the first botanist to try to classify this tree, he unfortunately mistook it for eastern dogwood. The first person to recognize it as a new species was the botanist Thomas Nuttall—but that is only part of the story. Nuttall records, 'On arriving...in 1834, at Ft. Vancouver, I hastened...to examine the productions of the forest of the Far West; and...the magnificent appearance...of this beautiful cornus.'

He was traveling with Dr. John K. Townsend, an ornithologist who treated 2 Native American children sick with 'intermittent fever.' Lacking quinine, Townsend made a brew from the bark of the dogwood. 'The second day they escaped the paroxysm and on the third day were completely well.' Native American peoples today still value this bark medicine as a blood purifier for stomach problems.

Townsend sent a specimen of the band-tailed pigeon to John James Audubon, the famed bird artist, who was also a friend of Nuttall. Townsend suggested that the painting of the bird might portray a dogwood with berries, a favored food of this pigeon. Audubon completed the painting and recorded that in it was 'a superb species of dogwood, discovered by our learned friend, Thomas Nuttall, Esq., when on his march toward the shore of the Pacific, and which I have graced with his name!'

CASCARA

Rhamnus purshiana

Cascara is a small tree, to just 9 m (30') tall, sometimes quite erect and sometimes quite ungainly. Looking to this tree for clues can leave you quite clueless. Even though it is unique among northwestern trees in having naked buds with only a covering of brownish hairs, this clue is not too noticeable to the average observer either.

The **clusters of small, greenish flowers** of late spring generally go unnoticed and the **plump, black berries** of late summer don't attract much attention. However, once you recognize the **alternate, prominently veined leaves**, 5–15 cm (2–6") long, then cascara appears to you quite frequently in the deciduous forest picture. It is often with red alder (see p. 64).

Lewis recorded it in 1806 on the banks of the Kooskoosky River (now the Clearwater) in Idaho. Sometime in the distant past aboriginal peoples discovered that the bark had definite medicinal qualities.

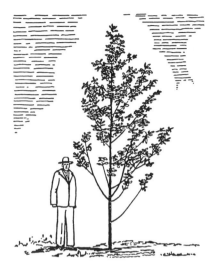

Franciscan missionaries in California learned of this discovery and called the tree *Cascara sagrada* ('holy tree'). By the 1880s its medicinal value was well established and cascara extracts became a product of Parke, Davis & Co. Much later the company produced for the U.S. Armed Forces a standard medication known as 'c.c. pills.' Surely one of these *c*'s stands for 'constipation,' for *Cascara sagrada* is regarded as a proven safe and effective laxative.

This tree came to public attention during World War II, when there was a great demand for the bark. The woods were scoured by 'chittom' bark peelers and most old-growth trees were cut. The bark was stripped from the trunk and larger limbs. It sold for about 20 cents a pound, big money in those near-Depression days. Now about 3 million pounds of bark is harvested annually.

Range: Wide-ranging, in mixed forest stands across the state. Fastest growth below 750 m (2500'), in shady coastal woods. Often among new growth in logged-over areas.

In May of 1826, Douglas made 2 crossings of an icy cold river in northern Washington by swimming and carrying his belongings. Then, almost frozen, he noted that it was '...very rainy during the whole night. I felt cold, my blanket and clothing being wet. As I could not sleep I rose at two o'clock and with some difficulty dried my blanket and a spare shirt, in which I placed my few plants....'

PACIFIC CRABAPPLE
Malus fusca

Usually a small, scraggly tree to 9 m (30') tall and 30 cm (12") in diameter. Old trees may be double that. Often shrub-like, with a number of stems about 5 cm (2") in diameter. Look for its **rather dense, rounded outline** in lowlands, marshes and wet meadows. It is often within 100 m (300 ft) or so of salt water. In late spring it carries clusters of **fragrant white-to-pinkish 'apple' blossoms, 5–12 in each flat-topped cluster**. By late July they have turned into **bunches of oblong little apples**, about 1.3 cm (1/2") long. Greenish at first, the **fruits become yellowish or blushed with red**. They are edible, but acidic. Coastal Native Americans used large quantities for food, either fresh or after being kept stored in water. Birds find them a good winter food.

The **leaves are much like those of a domestic apple**, but often with irregular lobes, all being sharply toothed and heavily veined. They turn beautiful shades of yellow and russet in autumn.

This tree was first identified by Archibald Menzies in 1792, at Port Discovery, about 15 km (10 mi) east of Sequim. He was with Captain George Vancouver, who was attempting to map Puget Sound. Menzies, eager and enthusiastic, went ashore at every opportunity.

The wood is very compact and fine grained. It is used in various small and specialty articles.

Range: An important clue! Low, damp places often close to the ocean. San Juan Islands and coastal strip. Ranges to over 600 m (2000') in elevation.

Lewis, December 1, 1805, 'There is a wild crab-apple which the natives eat...the fruit consists of little oval berries which grow in clusters at the end of twigs...when the fruit has been touched by frost it is not unpleasant.'

Lewis, January 28, 1806, 'The light brown berry is the fruit of this tree about the size and appearance in every respect with that of the U. States called the wild crabapple. The wood...is excessively hard when seasoned...I have seen the natives drive the wedges of this wood into solid dry pine....We have also found this wood useful to us for ax handles as well as glutts or wedges.'

Clark, March 26, 1806, '...they [the natives] substitute [for tobacco] the bark of the wild crab which they chew; it is very bitter.'

BLACK HAWTHORN
Crataegus douglasii

This species appears as either a **small, bushy tree** to 6 m (20') tall or a **shrubby tangle** that forms an impenetrable thicket. Although its **needle-sharp spines**, to 3 cm (1 1/4") long, are stressed in many descriptions, they can easily go unnoticed unless you make a close inspection. Far more noticeable during April and May are the **showy white clusters of blossoms**. These accurately mark the location of the tree or shrub in the dense growth along some roadsides. Flowers are about 1 cm (3/8") across, with 5 distinct petals.

By late July, the flowers are followed by clusters of **small, black-purple 'apples'** that wither soon after ripening. Although edible, the rough seeds make them unpopular today, but at one time they were eaten by coastal aboriginal peoples, either fresh or dried.

Leaves are thickish, oval and 7.5 cm (3") long. The **leaf margin is toothed**

all around and the top two-thirds of the leaf has
5–9 small lobes. The wood is tough and dense and
so was favored by aboriginal peoples for making small
implements. The stout thorns had uses whenever a
hard, sharp point was required. The legendary giant
lumberjack, Paul Bunyan, used a big hawthorn tree as
a back-scratcher.

Magpies build bulky nests in the thorny limb tangles. Hidden by leaves during summer, their location
is quickly noted when the leaves fall.

Note: Don't confuse black hawthorn, which has
spines, with Pacific crabapple, p. 56.

**Range: Low to middle mountain elevations. San
Juan Islands, coastal and ponderosa pine ecosystems. Okanogan, Chelan and Kittitas counties.
Also Spokane and Whitman counties.**

COMMON HAWTHORN
Crataegus monogyna

Spiny limbs, deeply lobed leaves
and colorful red berries that
persist over winter.

**Range: A widespread European
escape on the San Juan Islands
and southward.**

*Douglas, June 1825, 'The luxury of
a night's sleep on a bed of pine
branches can only be appreciated
by those who have experienced a
route over a barren plain, scorched
by the sun, or fatigued by groping
their way through thick forest,
crossing gullies, dead wood, lakes,
stones....'*

BIGLEAF MAPLE

Acer macrophyllum

A native tree that poses no problem in identification in its wide range, but around settlement it may mix with horticultural varieties. In the open, it is a massive, bushy tree with huge, spreading limbs but growing among other trees, it can be straight and free of limbs for a considerable distance, and it can be 37 m (120') tall. A trunk over 1.2 m (4') in diameter is not uncommon. The **leaves, which can reach 40 cm (16") across, are commonly 15–25 cm (6–10")—the largest of any tree** native to the state. A large bigleaf maple is a beautiful sight in fall, when its **typical 'maple' leaves, with 5 distinct lobes, turn golden-yellow**.

In spring, showy masses of **pale yellow flower clusters**, favored by bees and insects, stand out from afar and, with the forming leaves, give this maple a 2-toned color. By August, **pairs of seeds with large wings**, at an angle of 45–60°, have formed. They spin as they fall and in a breeze can travel a considerable distance. This tree is **often draped in moss and ferns** so thick as to obscure the limb structure—licorice fern is a prominent one. This drapery increases with the trees nearest to the coast and reaches its most spectacular proportions in the Hoh Valley of the Olympic Peninsula.

The wood is fine grained and very suitable for furniture, interior finishing and other specialty uses.

Also known as: broadleaf maple, Oregon maple.
Range: Mostly west of the Cascades at elevations under 300 m (1000'). Through the Columbia Gorge as far east as The Dalles, Oregon. Scattered occurrence along some water courses in Chelan and Klickitat counties.

Although Archibald Menzies, surgeon-botanist on Captain Vancouver's expedition of 1792, collected it and Lewis and Clark did likewise in 1805, and David Douglas gathered seeds around 1825 for shipment to England, none gave it a name. It remained for Thomas Nuttall, while professor of botany at Harvard, to name this tree and provide a technical description.

Clark, February 10, 1806, 'There is a tree common to the Columbia River [lower 160 km (100 mi)]. This tree is frequently 2 & 3 feet in diameter and rises to 50 or 60 feet. The froot is a winged seed and somewhat like the maple.'

DOUGLAS MAPLE
Acer glabrum

The great botanist Sir William Hooker named this tree after David Douglas.

As a small, upright tree, Douglas maple grows to 7.5 m (25') tall. However, it is **usually more shrub-like in form**, with a number of slender stems, and in some habitats it is often dwarfed. Leaves are small, 2.5–7.5 cm (1–3") wide, with **3–5 toothed lobes**. They are dark green, sometimes marked with red blotches. **In autumn the leaves turn a beautiful red** and contribute more of this color to the landscape than any other tree east of the Cascades.

The seed wings are very quick growing and prominent in late spring, when they tend to have a pinkish coloration. These **seed wings have very little spread**, making them

quite different from those of other native maples. The wood is hard and tough and, although limited in size, it was a favorite of Native American peoples, who used it for snowshoe frames and various utensils.

Range: Widespread at middle elevations east of the Cascades, often associated with ponderosa pine areas. Sporadic occurrences in rocky, open sites in Puget Sound.

VINE MAPLE
Acer circinatum

The early French *coureur de bois* (runners of the woods) called vine maple *bois de diable* (wood of the devil) for tripping them up on a portage or while they were 'breaking trail' through coastal forests.

The stems of this maple may stretch along the ground before they tilt upright to form a dense thicket. Often a small tree, but seldom with a single trunk. **Leaves are opposite, with 7–9 short, sharply toothed lobes that** look like blunt fingers. The **seed wings are widely spread—almost fully open**. Vine maple is a **blaze of red and yellow foliage in autumn**, the most vivid of all shrubs and trees in Washington.

Range: Lower to middle elevations from B.C. to California. Very noticeable on western sides of main mountain passes, especially when showing autumn colors. Olympics. Sporadic occurrences in wetter places east of the Cascades. Lake Chelan, Leavenworth, Mt. Rainier.

Lewis, 1805 or 1806, noted this maple 'on the great rapids of the Columbia River [in the area of the Great Falls, later known as Celilo Falls and since flooded].'

Douglas, June 1825, in the same area, 'At the Rapids an almost incredible number of salmon are caught...a scoop net...fastened around a hoop at the end of a long pole....The loop is made of acer circinatum.' A year later, 'Acer circinatum forms the underwood, a small hatchet or large knife...is indispensable.'

RED ALDER
Alnus rubra

What's red about this tree? A piece of cut bark will turn a bright orange. This phenomenon might be a clue, because alder is one of the great dye plants. It can produce a number of colors.

Groves of **slender, tall trees** with a noticeably **white-grayish bark marked with darker blotches**. It also grows in vigorous thickets on raw gravel soils. Look very closely at one of the dull **green leaves**. Note the large, blunt teeth and **leaf margins that are minutely rolled under**—positive identification. In spring, the male flowers appear as long, brown catkins to 10 cm (4") in length. By autumn, clusters of small, hard, brown cones about 1.3 cm (1/2") long have formed. Leaves drop while still green. Alders enhance soil fertility by having in their roots bacteria that convert nitrogen from the air into a form that alders and other plants can use.

Once a 'weed tree,' it is now the most important hardwood in the state. The basis for much of today's furniture, alder is also a good pulp wood and excellent for fuel. Leaves and bark had food and medicinal uses for aboriginal peoples. The bark contains 'salicin', a substance still used as medicine today.

Range: Mostly at lower elevations west of the Cascades. Infrequent on eastern slopes.

WHITE ALDER
Alnus rhombifolia

In creek bottoms it may attain a height of 18 m (60') and 30 cm (12") in diameter. Leaves, 5–9 cm (2–3 1/2") long, are half the length of the red alder's. The bark is scaly or plate-like.

Range: Note its limited range! The only alder in the dryland tributaries of the Snake and Columbia rivers in southeastern

Washington. May extend northward in arid areas to near the Okanogan River in north-central Washington.

MOUNTAIN ALDER
Alnus tenuifolia

At higher elevations, sprawling and shrub-like. In valleys, a tree to 12 m (40') tall and 30 cm (12") in diameter. The best identifying features are the buds—blunt and short-stemmed—and the **dull green leaves**. The **leaves are distinctly double-toothed, with definite sharp teeth. Catkins are almost stemless**.

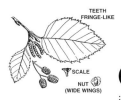

Range: The common, *widespread alder of mountain forests, generally found east of the Cascades. A good indicator of water.*

SITKA ALDER
Alnus crispa var. *sinuata*

TEETH
FRINGE-LIKE

SCALE

NUT
(WIDE WINGS)

Often a sprawling shrub to 3 m (10') tall, with crooked, upward-curving limbs. Buds are sharp-pointed and stemless. **Leaves are shiny above and have irregularly and sharply toothed leaf margins that are not rolled under**, but those of red alder are. Catkins are almost stemless.

Range: Usually *on higher mountain slopes and avalanche slides*, where it is a misery to hikers. Also at lower elevations, where it is generally along streams, marshes and wetlands. A good indicator of water.

BITTER CHERRY
Prunus emarginata

A confusing tree to identify in spring because of other road-side blossoms. Some are cherry and apple orchard escapees, others are hawthorns, pp. 58–59, and crab-apples, p. 56. **Count the blossoms!** Bitter cherry usually has **about 6 blossoms in each flat-topped cluster**, though there may be 5–10. The white-to-pink, **fragrant blooms appear from April to May**. By July, look for clusters of **bright red cherries** with a bitter taste. A slender, upright tree to 18 m (60') tall, with straight, upward-pointing branches—or a low, crooked shrub that forms a small thicket.

As with other cherries, young trees have **shiny reddish-brown bark with horizontal rows of raised lenticels**. On older trees these features aren't so noticeable. In spring, the leaf has 2 glands at the base of the stem. Leaves are finely toothed and may be up to 10 cm (4") long. The wood has little commercial value, but the colorful bark was used by Native Americans for decorative purposes in weaving and basket-making.

FLOWER CLUSTER

COAST

INTERIOR

Note: Sweet cherry, p. 67, is very showy and abundant.

Range: West of the Cascades at up to 900 m (3000') in elevation and mostly along streams. East of the Cascades it is usually found in the ponderosa pine ecosystem. Yakima, White Pass, Blue Mountains.

SWEET CHERRY
Prunus avium

A Eurasian import now well established in coastal areas. A tree to 18 m (60') tall with showy clusters of **white blossoms to 2.5 cm (1") across**, twice the size of bitter cherry blossoms. Blooms in April. Leaves finely toothed and sharply tipped.

Range: Puget Sound and southward. Hood Canal, Everett.

CHOKE CHERRY
Prunus virginiana

Often shrub-like, to 3 m (10') tall. Easily overlooked amid other growth except during May, when it is showy with dense **cylindrical flower clusters** about 10 cm (4") long. Note the **dark green, finely toothed leaves**, which are widest above their centers. When the

fruit is still red it is fairly eye-catching but, when ripe and black in late summer, it is hidden in the dark foliage. Leaves are considered poisonous because they contain cyanide.

The name of the choke cherry is significant if you link it to the puckery taste. Nevertheless, some people prize the fruit for jams and jellies. Native Americans especially, east of the Cascades, long ago picked the abundant berries and mixed them with meat to make pemmican, a food that could be stored for months.

Range: Damp ground, but also dry hillsides. East of the Cascades it is associated with ponderosa pine.

Lewis, May 29, 1806, 'The Choke Cherry has been in blume since the 20th inst.' Lewis and Clark were in Idaho, now on their return journey. Lewis devotes a page in his diary to a detailed description of the flower, demonstrating his expert botanical knowledge.

BLACK COTTONWOOD
Populus balsamifera ssp. *trichocarpa*

The black cottonwood is the **largest poplar** in North America and possibly in the world. This fast-growing and short-lived tree of valley bottoms often has rugged, stately trunks to over 90 cm (3') in diameter and 37 m (120') tall. Several in coastal areas have been measured at over 2.1 m (7') in diameter and to 41 m (135') tall. Giving a rich green border to many of our streams and rivers, providing a snowfall of cottony seeds in late spring and displaying its golden dress in autumn, it is a widespread treasure of the outdoors. Male and female flowers are on separate trees. The female flower matures into a **10 cm (4") long string of green beads**. They split to set adrift a cloud of tiny seeds, each with its own filmy parachute.

Young trees up to 15 m (50') tall have smooth, green bark and a conical form. They are quite unlike mature trees, with their thick, furrowed bark and ragged, heavily branched appearance. Leaves are roughly triangular in shape, finely toothed and with a lighter undersurface. Young trees might be confused with trembling aspen, p. 70, but note the difference in leaf shape: the leaves of trembling aspen are smaller and rounded or heart-shaped. Aspen leaves flutter in a breeze while those of the cottonwood simply turn and show a different green color. During spring, **large, resinous, sticky buds** perfume the air with a strong, pleasant balsam scent.

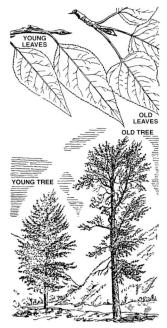

Cottonwood, with its soft, white wood, has a high value for pulp, veneer and plywood. Commercially, it is a very valuable broadleaf tree. However, if in contact with the soil, the cut wood quickly rots.

The various uses by Native Americans are legendary. All tribes gathered the sweet cambium layer, which was eaten 'as is.' Anyone touching one of those sticky buds could guess that they would be good as an ointment or a glue. Indeed, they were boiled and used in preparations for a multitude of woes. Interior tribes would fashion canoes from cottonwood and use its bark for cordage, baskets and fish traps.

Range: Generally confined to streamsides and riverbanks and low-lying lands, but will range to 1350 m (4400') in elevation. Large trees on eastern slopes of Olympics. East of Cascades along most watercourses.

How did such a prominent tree escape being named by Menzies, Lewis and Clark, or Douglas? Apparently it was another early botanist, William Hooker, who placed it on the records much later, in 1852, through providing a technical botanical description.

Clark, October 30, 1805, 'High mountains on either side, rugged and covered with...Pine Spruce Seder Cotton wood oake.' He was north of Beacon Rock, about midway through the Columbia Gorge.

TREMBLING ASPEN
Populus tremuloides

To identify, note the **slender trunk, dramatic whitish bark** often marked with black splotches, and the **small, rounded or heart-shaped leaf** with its **long stem flattened at right angles to the leaf blade**. Leaves are a fresh green color and **tremble in just a slight breeze**. Younger black cottonwood trees may have a long, white trunk, but

their leaves are large and triangular and do not tremble or twinkle.

Trembling aspen, although a comparatively small tree, finds stature in being the **most widespread tree** in North America. It ranges across the continent from the Pacific to the Atlantic. From near the Arctic Circle, where it is dwarf-sized, it decorates the landscape southward to northern Mexico. The altitudinal range is impressive, too: from sea level to near timberline in the Rockies.

Depending on site conditions, aspen may form a stately grove of trees to more than 40 cm (16") in diameter and 44 m (145') tall. **Bark is usually chalky-white and will not peel.** In many areas aspen forms beautiful clumps with trees of varying sizes because it clones itself from spreading roots. A mountainside with a patchwork of evergreens and groves of aspen in autumn color is a treasure of nature. Autumn aspen leaves are golden, those of black cottonwood a dull yellow.

Although aspen is a short-lived tree with a soft wood, it serves a purpose as a handy utility wood around ranches. It makes a high grade of excelsior (shavings) used for various packing purposes. And, when mixed with other woods, it provides a special grade of pulp used for magazines and books. Other uses include clipboards and firewood.

The spring cambium layer is soft and sweet at a certain stage and some aboriginal peoples used it as a ready-to-eat food. Aspen is also a favorite food of the beaver. Moose and snowshoe hares depend on the buds to help them survive winter. Woodpeckers drill aspen easily and small birds, such as swallows and bluebirds, nest in these holes.

Also known as: quaking aspen.
Range: Usually associated with ponderosa pine regions, but also ranges higher. Wide range does not include sagebrush or subalpine ecosystems. Spokane County, Blue Mountains and Bickelton. There is spotty growth of it in the San Juan Islands, usually in open areas near the ocean, but it is not found on the Olympic Peninsula.

Archibald Menzies, June 12, 1792, '...the Woods here [Birch Bay] abounded with the white & trembling Poplars together with black Birch. In consequence of discovery...the place afterwards obtained the name Birch Bay.'

PACIFIC WILLOW
Salix lucida ssp. *lasiandra*

Trying to identify willows can be very confusing. A willow may be a tree or a shrub. Ranges overlap and comparisons of leaf size, shape and color are frequently inconclusive. Often the flowers and fruits, which might offer clues, aren't on the tree when you are interested in identifying it. The 4 tree willows on pp. 72–74 have the widest range and are the ones most commonly seen and recognizable by leaf features, habitat and range. Note that in winter the bud of a willow is enclosed by a single overlapping scale.

Perhaps a slender tree or one with a more noticeable trunk to 40 cm (16") in diameter that soon forks into stout, crooked limbs thereby creating a tall, shaggy tree. The lance-shaped **leaf tapers to a long tip that often has a sideways twist**. They grow to 20 cm (8") long. The alternate **leaves are shiny and dark green above but smooth and whitish below**—a good identification feature. **Margins are distinctly toothed**, very finely on young leaves. Look for small wings (stipules) at base of leaf stem and several glands on upper leaf stem at base of leaf blade. **Twigs are yellowish-green.**

'EARS' ON YOUNG LEAVES

TWIST AT
LEAF END →

Also known as: shining willow, black willow.

Range: Wide-ranging, from sea level to lower mountain slopes. Most abundant west of the Cascades. May grow with cottonwood and red alder.

PEACH-LEAF WILLOW
Salix amygdaloides

Much like Pacific willow but leaf tips not twisted and no glands at base of leaf blade. Thin, drooping, yellow branchlets. Leaves finely toothed; pale green above, lighter beneath.

Range: Lakeshores and riversides, Okanogan Valley and southward into central Washington.

CRACK WILLOW
Salix fragilis

A European import with leaves like peach-leaf. 'Crack' because the fragile twigs snap or crack off easily. A windstorm will leave a litter of them behind.

Range: East of the Cascades. Usually seen as a row of very large trees along ditches, streams or bordering farmlands.

SCOULER'S WILLOW
Salix scouleriana

M ay be shrubby, but **usually a massive, sprawling tree** with a trunk diameter of 0.3–1.5 m (1–5'). The trunk soon branches into sprawling, twisting, heavy limbs. A rounded outline is formed, with a height of up to 14 m (45'). Usually the lower outline of the tree is lost in a thick growth of low shrubbery. East of the Cascades it may appear as a tall shrub with several stems from a common base. Stout, **hairy catkins ('pussy willows') appear before the leaves**. The **leaves are a dark green above and a light bluish-green beneath**. They are up to 13 cm (5") long. Most have a round-pointed tip, but a few may be sharply pointed. Important as a food source to deer and elk.

Range: The common willow of lower coastal elevations, moist bottomlands and sidehills. Widespread to elevation of 2150 m (7000').

OREGON ASH
Fraxinus latifolia

Until you become familiar with this tree, its form and its habitat, it will be difficult to locate among alders, bigleaf maples and cottonwoods. The first clue is to **associate it with wet areas, sloughs, creeksides, etc**. Even in April, when most other trees are in fresh leaf, Oregon ash looks like a dead tree among them. Later in spring, if it has lots of space, it can be a heavily foliated tree to 15 m (50') tall, with a rounded outline. Where its horizontal growth is restricted by other trees, it can grow to 23 m (75') tall, with a narrow top of compact branches.

Leaves are opposite and carry 5–7 leaflets. The bark is thick and ridged. Smaller ridges slant, giving a **woven effect to the bark. Small flowers precede the leaves**. By late summer, female trees display large clusters of **single-winged fruit**. In early autumn, before most other deciduous trees change color, **leaves turn a clear yellow**. The wood is of some commercial value: it is a favored hardwood for furniture, interior finishing and tool handles. Native Americans valued it for canoe paddles.

Range: **West of the Cascades, from sea level to near 900 m (3000'). Usually near water, in rich soils. Abundant in King, Snohomish and Clark counties. Southern Skamania County.**

Clark, October 31, 1805, '...a wet disagreeable evening, the only wood we could get to burn on this little Island on which we have encamped is the newly discovered Ash, which makes a tolerable fire...we made fifteen miles today.'

HACKBERRY
Celtis reticulata

A small tree seldom over 9 m (30') tall. In winter and early spring it is an unattractive mass of dead-looking limbs that persists after most other trees have come into leaf. Leaves are thick, dull green and to 7.5 cm (3") in length. They are rough to the touch and have a network of veins on the underside. Note that the **sides of a leaf are of unequal lengths**, like hackberry's close relatives, the elms. **Tiny, inconspicuous flowers** are followed by **single, cherry-like fruits**. They are edible but of poor eating quality, though birds find them quite satisfactory.

Range: *Usually associated with dry, rocky hillsides* **and often grows beside a huge boulder. Also along the courses of streams and rivers. Common in south-eastern Washington, on dry, rocky banks of the Snake River and the Columbia River and their trib-**  **utaries. Frequently seen along roadsides east of The Dalles. Noticeable around Clarkston, Pomeroy and Dayton. Dry Falls.**

Clark, October 12, 1805, '...open plains, no timber of any kind, a fiew hackberry bushes....So that fire wood is very scarce.'

CALIFORNIA WAX-MYRTLE
Myrica californica

A small tree or a sturdy shrub in coastal Washington. At the seashore, in the face of prevailing winds, it mixes with the salal backing the beach debris. Inland a short distance and protected from the wind, it may grow to tree form, to about 6 m (20') tall. Leaves are broadleaf and evergreen, 5–7.5 cm (2–3") long, shiny above, and olive-green beneath. Small, knobby catkins form in the leaf axils.

Note: Sweet gale, *Myrica gale*, is a shrub (see p. 119).

Also known as: curl-leaf mahogany.
Range: From Grays Harbor southward, near the ocean. Common in the Long Beach region.

MOUNTAIN MAHOGANY
Cercocarpus ledifollius

Sometimes a much-branched shrub to 4.5 m (15') tall, but may be tree-like, to 6 m (20') tall and with a trunk to 25 cm (10") in diameter. The name comes from the hard, mahogany-colored wood. The small leaves barely cover the spindly limbs. Leaves vary from 1.3 to 3 cm (1/2–1 1/4") long and have margins tightly rolled over. The lower surface is covered with a mat of yellowish hairs. From 1 to 4 hairy flowers form in the axils of the leaves; they change into spectacular seeds with long, silky tails.

Also known as: cut-leaf mahogany.
Range: Very limited. Dry, open ridges from 1500 m (5000') to 1850 m (6000') elevation in the Blue Mountains.

PAPER BIRCH
Betula papyrifera var. *papyrifera*

There are several varieties of paper birch, but only one is described here. This variety has been selected because it is the most numerous and because of its size and beautiful white bark. It is a tree likely to catch the eye. The image of the birch-bark canoe in the rapids, carrying Native Americans, trappers or fur-traders, is part of our heritage. A canoe weighing only 23 kg (50 lb) could carry 20 times its weight. Paper birch was as valuable a tree to Native Americans in eastern North America as redcedar was to western tribes.

Paper birch may stand as a specimen tree to 30 m (100') tall and 40 cm (16'') in diameter. More often it grows as a collection of several lesser, slanting trunks that root from a common base. The **bark separates into thin, papery layers, which are creamy or pinkish**. They are marked by segments of dark, horizontal lines. Although the bark appears fragile, it will outlast the core of a fallen tree. Even so, the wood is hard and strong and very valuable in the furniture trade. **Most leaves are wedge-shaped at the base and sharp-pointed at the tip** and grow to 7.5 cm (3'') long. **Twigs are smooth**, whereas those of water birch, p. 79, are warty.

Aboriginal peoples had uses for every part of this tree, with the possible exception of the roots. They knew how to make the sap flow, which they collected and used as a tonic, and they ate the inner bark (rich in vitamins and minerals). Young leaves and catkins were also eaten. The sheets of bark were fashioned into canoes and baskets.

Also known as: white birch, canoe birch.
Range: Northwestern Washington, as far south as Everett, where you can see tree clumps in pastures. Continues across the northern third of the state eastward into Idaho. The best growth is in Pend Oreille County, where it is abundant along streams, rivers and lake edges.

WATER BIRCH
Betula occidentalis

This tree often loses most of its distinctiveness in brushy creek bottoms or riverside thickets that include red-osier dogwoods, willows and alders. The grayish bark of old trees gives little clue, but young trunks have a rich reddish-brown bark marked horizontally with light lenticels. This information will help you recognize it, as a graceful tree or a tree clump to 15 m (50') tall. Long catkins are very decorative during May as the leaves are developing. Leaves are 2.5–5 cm (1–2") long. The bark will not peel and the tree in general doesn't have any special uses.

Also known as: black birch, red birch.

Range: East of the Cascades, mostly in the northeast quarter of the state and southward in the ponderosa pine ecosystem. Almost always near streams or damp areas.

RUSSIAN OLIVE
Elaeagnus angustifolia

Russian olive forms a bushy-leaved tree, perhaps 10 m (33') tall. Many trees are almost round in shape, with lower branches sweeping the ground. The trunk and main limbs have a dark, fissured bark. Leaves are narrow, 10 cm (4") long, with the underside silvery and the upper sage-green. Olives, which are the size of small peanuts, matching the leaves in color, grow singly here and there along the branches. They are considered inedible, but much used by wildlife. This tree is used quite extensively in landscape planting in very dry areas. Found sporadically along roadsides. Quite common on lands bordering the Columbia and Snake rivers. Wenatchee, Sunnyside, Lyons Ferry.

ENGLISH HOLLY
Ilex aquifolium

Holly, as a cultivated tree, with its masses of red berries, looks quite at home and unmistakable in a garden. But, as an ill-shaped, berryless shrub on a coastal island, it is less familiar. A foreign visitor prowling the woods could easily assume that he had found a native shrub, for holly is abundant and widespread. Only the low and shrubby Oregon-grapes, pp. 132–33, have similar leaves. 'Misplaced' holly can be found at low elevations in the San Juan Islands.

EUROPEAN MOUNTAIN-ASH
Sorbus aucuparia

The most conspicuous mountain-ash, because of its height—up to 5 m (16')—and its showy plumes of creamy flowers, which are followed by large clusters of red berries. More than (usually) 13 leaflets per leaf is definite identification. Meadows, fields and roadsides.

Note: Native mountain-ashes are on p. 153.

BLACK LOCUST
Robinia pseudo-acacia

Native to the eastern U.S. but widely introduced locally because it will grow in inhospitable areas and because the durable wood was once valuable for firewood and fence posts. A stout, erect tree to 25 m (80') tall, with fissured, black bark. In winter, the top third is heavily draped with brown masses of pea-pod–like seed cases. In May, clusters of whitish-to-pink blossoms cover the tree. Black locust has spiny twigs. Be sure not to confuse with Oregon ash, p. 75. Common around farms, silted areas and streambanks. Most common east of the Cascades.

BOX-ELDER
Acer negundo

A large tree native to more easterly states. It differs from other maples, pp. 60–63, in having leaves divided into 3–7 leaflets. The fruit is a pair of long, wrinkled, winged seeds. Throughout western and eastern Washington, usually close to habitations.

LOMBARDY POPLAR
Populus nigra var. *italica*

The distinctive columnar shape allows identification without detailed checking of leaf shape, flowers and fruit. French landscape paintings feature this poplar as rows of tall, thin, conical trees bordering a road or meadow. In our region it is a favorite for similar landscaping. It grows quickly, up to 30 m (100') in height. Not easily confused with any other tree. Common at lower elevations across Washington.

SPURGE-LAUREL
Daphne laureola

Although spurge-laurel is a shrub, it has been included here because it is a locally abundant introduced species. A shrub reminiscent of rhododendrons, pp. 150–51, with its dark evergreen leaves in rough whorls. Stems are too rubbery to break. Small, yellow-green flowers develop into clusters of poisonous purple-black berries. Sporadic, any-where from backyards to forest openings. San Juan Islands and adjacent mainland. In places it is threatening to become a pest.

LIST OF SHRUBS

This is not a key! This is a list of shrubs in the order that they appear in this book. Each shrub is listed in only one category and thus is omitted from other likely classifications. Use this list as a way of locating and comparing the shrubs.

WILLOWS
Groundhugging
Sandbar

EDIBLE BERRIES
Blueberry,
 Alaskan
 oval-leaved
 dwarf
Huckleberry,
 blue-leaved
 red
 evergreen
Grouseberry
Blackberry,
 Himalayan
 evergreen
 trailing
Raspberry,
 red
 black

UNPALATABLE BERRIES
Currant,
 red-flowering
 golden
 squaw
 sticky
 stink
Gooseberry,
 black
 gummy
 wild

CREEPERS
Kinnikinnick
Squaw carpet
Twinflower

CLIMBERS
Clematis,
 white
 Columbia
Honeysuckle,
 western trumpet
 hairy

SMALL
Mountain-heather,
 pink
 yellow
 white
Crowberry
Cinquefoil, shrubby
Falsebox
Penstemon,
 shrubby
 Scouler's
 Davidson's

BOG/MARSH
Bog-laurel
Birch, scrub
Tea,
 Labrador
 trapper's
Hardhack
Sweet gale

SAGEBRUSH
Sagebrush,
 big
 rigid
Antelope-brush
Greasewood
Sagewort, prairie
Rabbit-brush,
 common
 green
Horsebrush, gray
Sage,
 Dorr's
 hop
Juniper, common

PONDEROSA
Poison-ivy
Poison-oak
Sumac, smooth

HERE AND THERE
Elderberry,
 red
 black
 blue
Rose,
 nootka
 baldhip

clustered
 dog
Oregon-grape,
 tall
 dull
 creeping
Thimbleberry
Salmonberry
Saskatoon
Hazelnut,
 beaked
 California
Mock-orange
Oceanspray
Dogwood, red-osier
Snowberry,
 common
 trailing
Ninebark,
 Pacific
 mallow
Ceanothus, redstem
Deerbrush
Snowbrush
Twinberry, black
Honeysuckle, Utah
Goatsbeard
Spirea,
 birch-leaved
 pyramid
Soopolallie

COASTAL
Devil's club
Broom, Scotch
Gorse
Lupine, bush
Manzanita, hairy
Salal
Indian plum
Rhododendron, Pacific

MOUNTAINS
Rhododendron, white flowered
Copperbush
Azalea, false
Spirea, subalpine
Mountain-ash,
 Sitka
 western

PHOTO KEY TO THE SHRUBS

willow spp.
p. 90

coyote willow
p. 91

Alaskan blueberry
p. 92

oval-leaved
blueberry
p. 93

red huckleberry
p. 94

blue-leaved
huckleberry
p. 94

evergreen
huckleberrry
p. 95

black huckleberry
p. 95

grouseberry
p. 96

Himalayan
blackberry
p. 96

evergreen
blackberry
p. 97

trailing blackberry
p. 97

red raspberry
p. 98

black raspberry
p. 98

red-flowering
currant
p. 99

golden currant
p. 100

squaw currant
p. 100

sticky currant
p. 101

wild gooseberry
p. 102

black gooseberry
p. 103

gummy gooseberry
p. 103

kinnikinnick
p. 104

white clematis
p. 106

Columbia clematis
p. 107

western trumpet
honeysuckle
p. 108

hairy honeysuckle
p. 109

pink mountain-
heather
p. 110

yellow mountain-
heather
p. 110

white mountain-
heather
p. 111

crowberry
p. 112

shrubby cinquefoil
p. 112

falsebox
p. 113

shrubby penstemon
p. 114

bog-laurel
p. 116

scrub birch
p. 116

Labrador tea
p. 117

trapper's tea
p. 117

hardhack
p. 118

sweet gale
p. 119

big sagebrush
p. 120

rigid sagebrush
p. 120

antelope-brush
p. 121

greasewood
p. 121

prairie sagewort
p. 122

**common
rabbit-brush**
p. 123

green rabbit-brush
p. 123

gray horsebrush
p. 124

Dorr's sage
p. 124

hop sage
p. 125

common juniper
p. 125

poison ivy
p. 126

poison oak
p. 127

smooth sumac
p. 127

red elderberry
p. 128

black elderberry
p. 128

blue elderberry
p. 129

Nootka rose
p. 130

baldhip rose
p. 131

clustered wild rose
p. 131

tall Oregon-grape
p. 132

dull Oregon-grape
p. 133

creeping Oregon-
grape
p. 133

thimbleberry
p. 134

salmonberry
p. 134

saskatoon
p. 135

beaked hazelnut
p. 136

California hazelnut
p. 136

mock-orange
p. 137

oceanspray
p. 138

red-osier dogwood
p. 138

common snowberry
p. 139

Pacific ninebark
p. 140

mallow ninebark
p. 140

redstem ceanothus
p. 141

deerbrush
p. 141

snowbrush
p. 142

black twinberry
p. 143

Utah honeysuckle
p. 143

goatsbeard
p. 144

birch-leaved spirea
p. 144

pyramid spirea p. 145	soopolallie p. 145	devil's club p. 146	Scotch broom p. 147

gorse p. 147	bush lupine p. 148	hairy manzanita p. 148	salal p. 149

Indian plum p. 150	Pacific rhododendron p. 150	white-flowered rhododendron p. 151	coppperbush p. 151

false azalea p. 152	subalpine spirea p. 152	Sitka mountain-ash p. 153	western mountain-ash p. 153

WILLOWS
Salix spp.

Almost any place you go, sea coast, river valley, mountain slopes and even alpine terrain, you will find willows and, just by casual observation, note that what you are seeing is probably a willow. With persistence and detailed field guides you can identify many of them. Identification may depend on buds, catkins (pussy willows), the amount of hair on the twigs and leaves, and a comparison of leaf shapes and colors, top and bottom.

Willows can be so small as to create a shrubby mat only a few centimeters (or inches) tall, their tiny leaves dwarfed by out-sized catkins—3 such species are grouped under **'ground-hugging dwarf'** willows. There are several shrub-like willows, all with narrow and tapering leaves, that are often a pioneering growth on sandbars and gravel—2 common ones are listed below as **'sandbar'** willows. For 4 willows that can reach **tree size**, see pp. 72–73.

Most people have marveled at the strength and flexibility of willow branches or 'whips.' No wonder that Native Americans valued willows and their bark in making cord and rope for nets, baskets and a variety of other purposes. Willow bark is very bitter and, along with the leaves, was found to contain a substance, salicylic acid, that became the basic ingredient of aspirin. It is concentrated in the inner bark. Willow leaves can be used as a first-aid treatment on cuts and bruises.

GROUND-HUGGING DWARF WILLOWS
Shrubby, mat-like; to 15 cm (6") tall.

CASCADE WILLOW
S. cascadensis

Lance-shaped leaves, pea-green, to 5 cm (2") long. Alpine, southern Cascades.

NETTED WILLOW
S. reticulata

Leaves round, strongly veined, to 1.3 cm (1/2") long. Widespread.

ARTIC WILLOW
S. arctica

Often prostrate. Gray-green leaves with a whitish bloom, to 5 cm (2") long. Not toothed. Cascades. **Subalpine to alpine**.

SANDBAR WILLOWS

Slender, to 4.5 m (15') tall.

COYOTE WILLOW
S. exigua

Leaves to 5–10 cm (2–4") long and 0.6 cm (1/4") wide. Silvery-green. A pioneer growth on **gravel bars**. East of Cascades.

SOFT-LEAVED WILLOW
S. sessilifolia

Leaves to 7.5 cm (3") long, glossy, pointed both ends. Coastal; from Fraser River (B.C.) bars southward to Columbia River.

BLUEBERRIES AND HUCKLEBERRIES
Vaccinium spp.

A species in the genus *Vaccinium* may be commonly known as a blueberry, huckle-berry, grouseberry, whortleberry, bilberry or cranberry, thus providing a great opportunity for confusion. Flower color varies from white to red. Berry color, generally the best identifying feature, ranges through shades of red to blue and black. Without flowers or berries available, species identification might be made using habitat, subtle differences in leaf or twig features, and overall size.

ALASKAN BLUEBERRY
Vaccinium alaskaense

A leaf of Alaskan blueberry, if turned over and bent lengthwise along the midvein, shows scattered hairs along the underside of the midvein. The oval leaves are 2–6.5 cm (3/4–2 1/2'') long. Pinkish-to-bronze **flowers with a protruding tip appear with or after the leaves**. The dark bluish-black **berries without bloom** are of good eating quality. This loosely branched shrub grows to 1.2 m (4') tall.

Note: This shrub closely resembles oval-leaved blueberry, p. 93, which is found in the same range.

FLOWER

BERRY

Range: West-facing slopes of the Cascades, from low to subalpine elevations. Widespread in moist, more open forests.

OVAL-LEAVED BLUEBERRY
Vaccinium ovalifolium

This plant is the tallest blueberry bush of all, commonly reaching 1.8 m (6'). Its scraggly form prefers shady places. Leaves about 4 cm (1 1/2") long are oval and rounded at both ends. The **pink blossoms are usually out before the leaves. The style does not protrude beyond the flower globe**. The bluish-black berries have a **bluish bloom**.

Note: Compare features with Alaskan blueberry, p. 92, which resembles this shrub.

Range: Widespread west of the Cascades in moist forest areas, from middle to subalpine elevations.

DWARF BLUEBERRY
Vaccinium caespitosum

Prized for its tasty berries. Usually **less than 20 cm (8") tall**. Bushy and so producing a mass of **finely toothed leaves, bright green on both sides**, the underside with a noticeable network of fine veins. Leaves vary from 0.6 to 2.5 cm (1/4–1") long and are widest above the center. Small, white-to-pink **flowers are distinctly urn-shaped**, but show 5 lobes. Flowers and berries are 1 per leaf axil. The **blue berries have a paler bloom**.

Range: Wide-ranging. Common in swamps and along damp mountain meadows and, for some reason, also on high, rocky ridges.

BERRY

RED HUCKLEBERRY
Vaccinium parvifolium

Unmistakable, with its **slender, upright branches**. Often 1.8 m (6') tall and decorated by a spaced growth of **oval, bright green leaves** less than 2.5 cm (1'') long. **Angled branches are as green as the leaves**. Often in the shade or filling a small opening, this shrub frequently perches on an old stump or log. The **bright red berries** are rather scattered and may be few indeed. Although a little tart to the taste, they make a fine dessert when cooked. Ripe in July. Native Americans prized them as a food to be dried and formed into cakes for winter use. More often eaten fresh.

Range: The most common low-elevation *Vaccinium* species in Washington. Generally found below 300 m (1000') elevation, growing among open-spaced forest trees or in clearings, on San Juan Islands and coastal slopes.

BLUE-LEAVED HUCKLEBERRY
Vaccinium deliciosum

To 30 cm (12'') tall and with a **definite bluish tinge to the leaves** that immediately identifies it. It can form **low, compact, shrubby mats** over extensive areas. **Small, round, pinkish flowers**, mostly 1 per leaf axil. Leaves less than 6 mm (1/4'') long, oval with a rounded tip. Blooms late July. **Berries blue with a pale bloom**. Excellent flavor.

Range: Subalpine meadows of Olympics and Cascades.

EVERGREEN HUCKLEBERRY

Vaccinium ovatum

This shrub has a 'hide-away' quality and is often lost in a vigorous growth of salal. Also note its limited range. Usually about 1.2 m (4') tall, it can be double that. It is erect and bushy, with **shiny evergreen leaves**, which make it unique among *Vaccinium*. **Leaves are finely toothed**, 2–5 cm (3/4–2") long and alternate, but have a 2-ranked appearance. During May into June, new twig ends may have a reddish tinge.

During May it displays clusters of **pink bell flowers**, slowly replaced by **shiny black berries**, which ripen in late summer but may hang on until December. Aboriginal peoples found these berries plentiful and ate them fresh or prepared them for later use by drying. Both the Lewis and Clark Expedition and David Douglas noted these berries and no doubt picked them when available.

Range: These bushes are most abundant close to the ocean and are a feature on the San Juan Islands, in the Olympics and in coastal Washington.

BLACK HUCKLEBERRY

Vaccinium membranaceum

A height of 1.5 m (5') is common at lower elevations, but this huckleberry becomes a low, shrubby growth in the subalpine where, in the early autumn, it turns into a beautiful purple carpet. **Leaves are very finely toothed**—it takes a close look! **Single, large, reddish-black berries without a bloom**. People pick them along mountain roads from late July to September.

Range: Often the *most common berry bush* at middle to subalpine elevations. Widespread across the state.

Lewis, February 7, 1806, '...the leaf is thin, of a pale green...serrated, but so slightly so that it is scarcely perceptible.'

GROUSEBERRY
Vaccinium scoparium

Another plant quickly recognizable by its **small, lacy, light green leaves** to 1.3 cm (1/2'') long. Usually bunched and forming a **carpet in the shade of trees at high elevations**. Small, red berries difficult to pick.

Range: High mountain slopes east of the Cascades. Chinook Pass, Wenatchee Mountains, Blue Mountains at 1850 m (6000').

HIMALAYAN BLACKBERRY
Rubus discolor; R. armeniacus

To many people this shrub will be the one recognized as a **common, horrendously armed vine**, decorated with either large clusters of white-to-pink blossoms or showy

branches of **red and black blackberries**. Sometimes during summer both flowers and berries can be seen on the vine at the same time.

Thick, arching branches to 3 m (10') long are heavily armed with **large, recurved spines**, a formidable hazard at berry-picking time in late July and August. **Berries are abundant** and valued for eating fresh or for making jams, jellies and pies. Officially, **blackberries are distinguished from raspberries by the fact that, when it comes off the vine, a blackberry still contains a white core and a raspberry leaves it behind**. Leaves have either 3 or 5 leaflets and some persist over winter.

Range: This foreign introduction is spreading rapidly and is now widespread at lower coastal elevations. It often grows along roads, over fences and against old buildings.

EVERGREEN BLACKBERRY
Rubus laciniatus

Often growing with Himalayan blackberry, and remarkably similar in form, flower and berries. However, this blackberry is immediately distinguishable by its **deeply cut and roughly toothed leaves. Leaves are evergreen**, although a number do fall. Berries from this one may slightly surpass those of the Himalayan in flavor and storage quality.

Range: Another introduction with range same as Himalayan blackberry, p. 96.

TRAILING BLACKBERRY
Rubus ursinus

Watch for a long, thin, blue-stemmed creeper, usually close to the ground or just high enough to catch a shoe and trip you. Small, recurved thorns along the stem add to the problem. Our only native blackberry. On male plants the white-to-pinkish flowers are larger, about 4 cm (1 1/2") across, than on the female ones, where they measure just 2 cm (3/4") across. Leaves, usually with deeply toothed, 3-lobed leaflets, are quickly recognized. The black and glossy fruit, a typical 'blackberry,' ripens in August and is much favored by humans, bears, birds and even deer.

Also known as: dewberry.
Range: Logged-over and burned areas. Edges of forests. Coastal Douglas-fir regions.

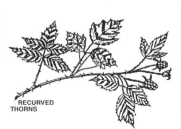

RECURVED
THORNS

97

RED RASPBERRY
Rubus idaeus

The shape and color of the red raspberry are familiar to most people. Shrub stems, often with a bluish bloom, are covered with thin thorns. To 1.5 m (5') tall. The leaves, with 3–5 leaflets,

THIN, STOUT SPINES

are white-powdery beneath. Berries are sweet when fully ripe.

Range: East of the Cascades, in dry places, such as the rockslides found in the bunchgrass and ponderosa pine ecosystems.

BLACK RASPBERRY
Rubus leucodermis

Very similar to the raspberry above in being a shrub to 1.5 m (5') tall. **Bristly with sharp spines**. The **crinkled leaves have a silvery undersurface and are divided into 3–5 leaflets**. Before they turn black, the **unripe berries resemble red raspberries**. A great favorite of berry pickers.

Note: Other plants—such as salmonberry, thimbleberry and saskatoon—have berries whose palatability depends on personal taste. These shrubs are in the grouping 'Here and There' (pp. 128–45).

Also known as: blackcap.
Range: In open forests and disturbed lands, at low to medium coastal elevations. Also, forests of eastern Washington.

Douglas, March 24, 1826 (at The Dalles), '...a fellow immediately pulled from his quiver a bow and a handful of arrows, and presented it at Mr. McLeod. As I was standing on the outside of the crowd I perceived it, and, as no time was to be lost, I instantly slipped the cover of my gun, which at the time was charged with buckshot, and presented at him, and invited him to fire his arrow, and then I should certainly shoot him...a chief stepped in...and settled the matter in a few words....This friendly Indian, who is the finest figure of a man I have ever seen, standing nearly 6 feet, 6 inches high....'

CURRANTS AND GOOSEBERRIES
Ribes spp.

Currants and gooseberries are easily differentiated: **currants do not have any spines or prickles but gooseberries are armed**. Although the currants listed in this book are classed as 'unpalatable,' some were used by Native Americans. All are generally of poor taste.

CURRANTS

RED-FLOWERING CURRANT
Ribes sanguineum

A beloved symbol of springtime at the coast, where by early April these shrubs are a **mass of red-flowered blooms**. The flowers coincide with the arrival of humming-birds to feed on the nectar. At this time of year there is nothing else to confuse with this bushy shrub. It varies in height, from only 1 m (3 1/2') to 3 m (10'). It grows erect, either compact in form or loose and spreading, depending on soil and light factors. Dull green leaves, 2.5–7.5 cm (1–3") across, have a mealy texture and are matted on the underside with very fine hair. The **5-petaled red flowers hang in clusters** for several weeks and disappear during May. The globular, **blue-black berries have a waxy bloom** and hang in loose clusters. In no way poisonous, they have an unpleasant taste.

Range: Widespread at lower elevations in drier areas of the coastal forest ecosystem. Occasional intrusions eastward.

David Douglas greatly admired red-flowering currant. He collected seed rather than cuttings and introduced it to European botanical gardens. It was soon a prized display. It is said that the sale of this shrub more than paid for Douglas's trip to the Pacific Northwest.

GOLDEN CURRANT
Ribes aureum

During April and May this shrub is not easily confused with anything else, but it rather loses itself once the blooming is over. When it is in bloom, you may see this currant on a rockslide or find it in the shade of trees in a valley bottom. The **small, yellow flowers are in clusters of 6–15**. They may have a red or purplish tinge. Match them with the **distinctive 3-lobed leaves** and you have 2 easy-to-remember characteristics for recognition. Usually 1.2–1.8 m (4–6') tall.

The **distinctive round, smooth berries are yellow, red or almost black** and about 6 mm (1/4") in diameter. Note the long, chalky protuberances on them.

Range: East of the Cascades, in areas with ponderosa pine or not far away. Wenatchee, Yakima, Spokane.

Lewis, April, 16, 1806, 'I also met with sundry other plants...a currant...now in blume and has [a] yellow flower.'

FLOWER

BERRIES

STINK CURRANT
Ribes bracteosum

Large 'currant' leaves to 20 cm (8") in length, wider than long, 5–7 sharp-tipped lobes. Erect, green-to-pink flowers, black fruit on long, loose clusters.

Range: low to alpine in coastal ecosystem.

Lewis, 1805 or 1806, found stink currant, 'On the Rocky-mountain in the interior of North America.'

Douglas noted that 2–3 berries will cause vomiting. He was short on food supplies during much of his travels. Likely he tasted most berries and so could comment from experience.

SQUAW CURRANT
Ribes cereum

This currant bush is quickly noticed in the dry regions east of the Cascades. Its bushy growth, to 1.2 m (4') tall, dots the lower slopes of rockslides and often grows against a large boulder. Its **small, broadly 3-lobed leaves are dime- to quarter-sized**. During May this shrub displays small clusters of **2–8 greenish-white flowers**. In July or August it is covered by **translucent bright red berries** 6–7 mm (1/4") in diameter. Although dry and tasteless, they were a food source for aboriginal peoples.

Range: Anywhere from the lower slopes of the ponderosa pine zone through the bunchgrass zone to sagebrush areas. Okanogan and Chelan counties and southward. Columbia River east of The Dalles.

David Douglas recorded its range as, '...river Columbia from the Great Falls [Cecilo Falls, now flooded, located 1.6 km (1 mi) downriver from Wishram] to the source of that stream in the Rocky Mtns.'

STICKY CURRANT
Ribes viscosissimum

Another very visible currant in early spring, but this one grows in semi-open forests and is often quite abundant over a large area. Most bushes are 0.6–1.2 m (2–4') tall. Books usually stress the sticky pores on the twigs, leaves and fruit as the most dominant feature, but they are less noticeable in spring as the flowers bloom. The greenish-white flowers are about 6 mm (1/4") long, often with a pinkish tinge, in a cluster of 6–12 blooms. They form the largest flower mass of all the currants. Berries are oval and bluish-black. They are dry and have a disagreeable taste and smell.

Range: From the Cascades eastward, on mountain slopes from 500–1850 m (1700–6000'). Ponderosa pine and mountain forest ecosystems. Ferry County, Sherman Pass.

GOOSEBERRIES

Remember, currants are unarmed. Gooseberries carry spines. Most of these plants are in flower April to May. Only the more common ones have been included.

WILD GOOSEBERRY
Ribes divaricatum

Stems are sturdy and often arching. **Leaf nodes have 1–3 spines. Flowers purple or greenish**. Sepals reflexed and stamens long and protruding. The large, purple berry is smooth, its edibility a matter of preference.

Range: A shrub of lower elevations. San Juan Islands, coastal forest area. Lower Columbia Gorge.

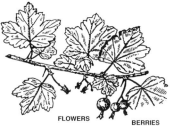

FLOWERS   BERRIES

BLACK GOOSEBERRY

Ribes lacustre

A shrub of damp, shady places about 1 m (3 1/2') tall with weakly upright, spiny stems. Look for small 'maple' leaves, 5-lobed and to 6.5 cm (2 1/2") wide. Bristly young stems carry **3–7 heavy spines at each leaf node**.

The main feature to catch attention is the **saucer-shaped flowers, tinged with maroon and red, hanging 5–12 in a cluster**. They are replaced by bristly, purple-black berries. It is a matter of opinion as to their taste. Some aboriginal peoples ate them, others avoided them as poisonous.

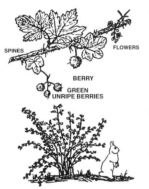

SPINES FLOWERS
BERRY
GREEN UNRIPE BERRIES

Also known as: black swamp gooseberry.
Range: Wide-ranging, from sea level to 1850 m (6000') in a variety of forest habitats. Olympics, Wenatchee and Blue mountains.

GUMMY GOOSEBERRY

Ribes lobbii

To about 2 m (6 1/2') tall. **'Gummy' refers to the stickiness of the leaves**. Like black gooseberry, above, gummy gooseberry has reddish flowers, but note the reflexed sepals and stamens that protrude beyond the tiny petals. Stamens are tipped with red or purple. Often **only 1–3 flowers plus usually 3 spines per leaf node**. Berries are black, sticky, bristly and coarse to the touch. Poor taste.

Range: Wide-ranging, from damp lowlands to mountain forests. Cascades, but most abundant on eastern slopes.

KINNIKINNICK
Arctostaphylos uva-ursi

A glossy evergreen, mat-like creeper. Usually on a thin, exposed rocky or gravelly soil, such as along an old roadside. Although some specimens might be only 1 m (3 1/2') across, kinnikinnick can cover an extensive surface as runners slowly extend. The **small, pinkish bell flowers** of spring can easily go unnoticed. However, a good display of **mealy, red berries** in late August and into September is more eye-catching. Berries are of poor eating quality. Leaves are alternate, leathery, and to 1.3–2.5 cm (1/2–1") long.

A number of western Native American groups have traditionally mixed the dried leaves with other leaves and barks to create a smoking mixture that became known as 'Indian tobacco.'

Arctostaphylos is from the Greek *arctos* (a bear) and *staphylos* (a bunch of grapes). *Uva-ursi*, from Latin, translates as 'berry-bear.'

Also known as: common bearberry.
Range: On exposed and well-drained soils across the state. Extends to sub-alpine elevations. In the interior cedar–hemlock ecosystem it is limited to rocky southern exposures.

Lewis, January 23, 1806, '...a scarletbury about the size of a small cherry...the clerks of these trading companies [Hudson's Bay Company] carrying the leaves of this plant in a small bag for the purpose of smoking of which they are exceedingly fond.'

Lewis, January 29, 1806, '...to me it is a very tastless and insippied fruit...the natives eat them without any prepation.'

BERRIES

'BELL' FLOWERS

SQUAW CARPET
Ceanothus prostratus

Can spread over a dry forest floor in a low carpet, sometimes to 3 m (10') across. Squaw carpet resembles kinnikinnick, but lacks red berries and has opposite (not alternate) evergreen leaves one-half the size, to just 1.3 cm (1/2") long. Coarsely toothed, giving leaf a 'holly' look, and comparatively thick. Very tiny flowers, white to blue, in twin bell-like clusters, each about 2 cm (3/4") across.

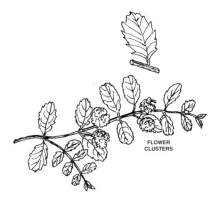

FLOWER CLUSTERS

Note: Other *Ceanothus* on pp. 141–42.

Range: Dry forests on eastern slopes of Cascades, Yakima south. Considered to be rather rare.

TWINFLOWER
Linnaea borealis

Although it looks like it should be considered as a wildflower, twinflower is technically classed as a shrub because of the thin, woody vine.

Spreading vines, perhaps 0.9–1.2 m (3–4') long, crawl over the forest floor. Little evergreen leaves are less than 1.3 cm (1/2") long and almost round; they are shiny, dark green above and much paler on underside. Teeth along upper half of leaves will clear up any identification problems. Occasionally a dense mat with hundreds of flowers.

In June and July, numerous flower stems each carry a white or pink 'twin' flower delicately scented. Linnaeus, famous Swedish botanist and founder of the current system of botanical classification, chose twinflower as his favorite plant.

Range: A common plant in cool, moist woods throughout, from sea level to timberline.

WHITE CLEMATIS
Clematis ligusticifolia

A blessing to anyone looking for it, this vigorous creeper advertises itself by climbing into shrubs and fences, where it displays **fluffy masses of small, white flowers**. The first blooming during May is prolonged with new growth and flowers. Former blooms become seed balls that rather resemble the flowers and may last past October. The stout vine can grow to a length of 15 m (50'), so it isn't unusual to see bloom or seed in strange places. The tough, stringy bark was peeled off and used in a variety of ways by Native Americans. It was woven with dogbane (*Apocynum* spp.) to make very strong and decorative products, such as mats, bags and rope.

Also known as: old man's beard, white virgin's bower. **Range:** East of the Cascades. Often associated with ponderosa pine, chokecherry and Saskatoon bushes. Common along road edges, old farm buildings, rocky outcroppings.

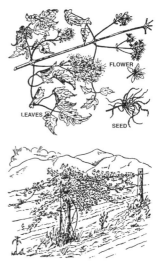

COLUMBIA CLEMATIS
Clematis occidentalis

Here's a plant to give you a thrill the first time you see it. The blue flowers, 5–10 cm (2–4") across, have an ethereal quality, especially since the slender vine that carries them is almost unnoticeable amongst other growth. The flower's **blue sepals, which look like petals, are set off by a yellow center**. This clematis blooms May into June. By the middle of summer, the flowers have miraculously turned into **fluffy, white 'dust mop' seedheads**.

Also known as: blue clematis, virgin's bower.
Range: Shady mountain slopes or valley bottoms east of the Cascades. Most common along upper edge of ponderosa pine ecosystem and into the mountain forests. Ferry County, Spokane. Roadsides west of Sherman Pass (east of Republic).

Lewis and Clark carried red, white and blue beads as trade items. They discovered that the Native Americans preferred the blue ones and were very adept at bargaining. Alexander Mackenzie, who in 1793 had reached the Pacific Ocean from the east using an overland route through what is now Canada, had commented on this preference, but his advice was ignored.

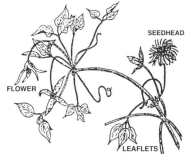

SEEDHEAD

FLOWER

LEAFLETS

WESTERN TRUMPET HONEYSUCKLE
Lonicera ciliosa

No mistaking this climber, for its several thin **stems spiral around trunks and branches**. Sometimes it will climb to a height of 9 m (30'). **Opposite oval, entire leaves**; the terminal pair make an irregular disk. Lower surfaces have a whitish bloom that easily rubs off.

During May and into June, **clusters of orange flowers, thin and tube-like**, attract attention and the rest of the plant fades into the background. In September, **clusters of translucent orange-red berries** take the stage. They are inedible and are filled with pulp and large seeds. Hummingbirds are attracted to the flowers, and many bird species enjoy the berries.

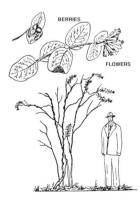

Also known as: orange honeysuckle.

Range: Abundant in drier forest areas below 600 m (2000') elevation west of the Cascades. Sporadic in eastern parts of the state. Pend Oreille and Spokane counties. Blue Mountains, Columbia Gorge.

HAIRY HONEYSUCKLE

Lonicera hispidula

A **slender, trailing plant** to 3.7 m (12') long that favors dry, open forests. **Stems are hairy and hollow**, but the **opposite, oval leaves are typical of the honeysuckles**. It blooms from middle to late summer and displays **pinkish-purple flowers** 1–2 cm (3/8–3/4") long. They have large, prominent stamens. The **red fruits** are considered inedible.

Also known as: purple honeysuckle.
Range: From San Juan Islands south-ward, in suitable habitats west of the Cascades.

David Douglas collected seeds, which were then grown in English gardens and arboretums. Most days he started his travels at dawn and was on the go for 3 or more hours before he had breakfast—as meager as it may have been. Then away again with some travel plan in mind.

Douglas, June 1, 1825, 'I killed two partridges [grouse]...which I placed in my little kettle to boil for supper....I awoke at daybreak and beheld my supper burned to ashes and 3 holes in the bottom of my kettle....I had to make a little tea. This I did by scouring out the lid of my tinder-box and boiling water in it.'

PINK MOUNTAIN-HEATHER
Phyllodoce empetriformis

A joy of the high country that every hiker hopes to find in bloom. One might find a single plant, a whole bed of heather or, on occasion, acre after acre! There is nothing with which to mistake its vibrant color. In bloom during July and August, the **hundreds of rose-pink bell blossoms** provide a floral spectacle. Europeans on holiday quickly recognize the similarity to the closely related heather or heath of their own countries.

Usually about 30 cm (12") tall, this shrubby mat is an **evergreen with alternate leaves** relatively short and needle-like.

Note: Compare to crowberry, p. 112, which is similar in form.

Also known as: red heather, red mountain-heather.
Range: At subalpine and alpine tundra elevations. Extends from Alaska to California. Olympics, Mt. Rainier, Mt. Baker. This plant was once named after Archibald Menzies, who, it is said, in the early 1790s recorded it on the 'West Coast of North America.'

YELLOW MOUNTAIN-HEATHER
Phyllodoce glanduliflora

For all intents and purposes, the same plant as the above, but with **creamy or whitish-green flowers**. Flowers cluster at the ends of flowering stems. Often it will be found growing with pink mountain-heather, a delightful combination of color. Hybridization is common and you may see a strange blending of colors.

Range: Same as pink mountain-heather, above.

WHITE MOUNTAIN-HEATHER

Cassiope mertensiana

Another common plant of the high country that grows in the same form and areas as the other mountain-heathers. The small, **white flowers are bell-shaped** and bloom in July and August. **Opposite, stemless leaves are arranged in 4 rows** and cling tightly to the stem.

Note: There are 2 other, closely related white-flowering mountain-heathers, *C. tetragona* and *C. stelleriana*, that range northward from Mt. Rainier.

Range: Subalpine and alpine tundra ecosystems.

FLOWERS

4 ROWS OF SCALY LEAVES

CROWBERRY
Empetrum nigrum

Outwardly resembles a mountain-heather, pp. 110–11, but quickly proven different by having **in the leaf axils small, purplish flowers or large, black berries**, as black as a crow. **The short leaves are thick and needle-like, grooved beneath**. The **berries are abundant, large and juicy**. Although edible, they never were a favorite with aboriginal peoples and are not to be compared with blackberries. Whereas mountain-heather favors dry, exposed slopes in the subalpine and alpine regions, crowberry is usually in partial shade and so grows at a lower level.

Range: Westward side of the Olympics, where it grows in damp, shady places from sea level to timberline. Otherwise from 900 m (3000') to timberline in the Cascades.

SHRUBBY CINQUEFOIL
Potentilla fruticosa

You can hike a lot of high country without seeing this shrub and then there it is, dotting a hillside or brightening a dry ridge. A small, sprawling shrub, often with a thick main stem. It may reach 90 cm (3') tall, but is more commonly half that height. The **yellow flowers resemble those of a buttercup in size and color, but don't have a waxy shine**. Many of this native plant's garden-ornamental relatives look much like it. Leaves are important to identification. The velvety **leaves have 3–7 leaflets; 5 is the usual number.**

Range: From the Cascades to the Rockies. Sporadic, in subalpine and alpine areas. Mt. Rainier National Park—see it at Frozen Lake, above the Sunrise Visitor Center. Olympics.

FALSEBOX
Paxistima myrsinites

A trim little evergreen plant that blends into the rest of the native greenery. The small, 4-petaled flowers usually go unnoticed and no berries are formed. In the forest, in damper ground, it may reach 90 cm (3') tall and be loose and sprawling. In subalpine areas it is usually a **compact, dark green shrub** that complements the flowers of other plants on dry, rocky ground. Check by noting the **small, evergreen leaves, to 2.5 cm (1") long, with distinct short teeth,** on thin, angled twigs.

Range: Widespread in damper coniferous forests, from sea level to the subalpine, where it prefers dry, rocky ground. A common roadside shrub in many places.

STEMS SQUARISH

PENSTEMONS
Penstemon spp.

There are many penstemons in Washington. The 3 mentioned here can be classified as shrubs because of their tough, woody stems. All 3 are also distinguished by **wooly-tipped anthers**.

SHRUBBY PENSTEMON
Penstemon fruticosus

Not mat-forming, but a shrub-like growth to 30 cm (12") tall. Leaves, mostly opposite, are short-stemmed and to 6.5 cm (2 1/2") long and 1.3 cm (1/2") wide. Leaf edges may be smooth or finely toothed. The long-tubed flowers are a bright blue-lavender or a pale purple. The **lower lip of the flower has white hair at its base**; the anthers are wooly-tipped. Blooms May to July.

Range: East of the Cascades to the Rockies. Common along steep roadsides. From low to high mountains, on open rocky slopes.

SCOULER'S PENSTEMON

Penstemon fruticosus var. *scouleri*

A twiggy, low, shrub-like growth with short flower stems. The **leaves are important to identification—usually finely toothed and about 6 mm (1/4") wide**. The flowers, in showy purple clusters, are about 4 cm (1 1/2") long. As with the other penstemons, the anthers are wooly-tipped. Blooms April to May.

Range: East of the Cascades. Very showy on steep banks and rocky places from low to subalpine.

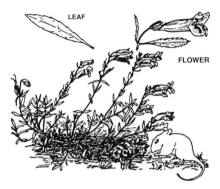

Douglas, July 1830, '...it was the 1st of July before I could leave the coast for the Interior, has been a serious drawback; the season proving unusually early, all the vernal plants, which are by far the most numerous, beautiful and curious here, were withered and decayed.'

DAVIDSON'S PENSTEMON

Penstemon davidsonii

A **mat-like growth of leaves**, with short, loosely branched **flower stems to 30 cm (12") tall**. The **distinctive evergreen leaves, to 6 mm (1/4") long**, may have small teeth. Leaves cluster into a tight mat. The long, blue-purple flowers, on very short stems, appear somewhat flattened. The flower throat is bristly and the wooly-tipped anthers are easily seen. Blooms June to August.

Range: In rocky places from middle to sub-alpine elevation throughout the state.

BOG-LAUREL
Kalmia microphylla ssp. *occidentalis*; *K. polifolia*

Always confined to boggy areas. Thin, twisting stems up to 60 cm (2') tall that can get lost in the thicker growth of Labrador tea. However, when the **rose-colored flowers** are out in May, you will find it quickly. Flowers are 1.3 cm (1/2") across and have 5 petals. The **10 stamens are bent back, and kept in place by the anthers at their tips being held in pits in the petals**. When an insect disturbs a stamen, the elastic stalk whips upward to spray the intruder with pollen.

The opposite, leathery leaves are less than 2.5 cm (1") long. **Leaves have edges strongly rolled over and a velvety whiteness beneath**. Compare with Labrador tea, p. 117, which has longer leaves with a rusty wool on the underside.

Also known as: American laurel, alpine kalmia, bog kalmia.

Range: Boggy places and wet meadows of the coast forest ecosystem.

SCRUB BIRCH
Betula glandulosa var. *glandulosa*

A loose, sprawling shrub that can reach 4.5 m (15') in height. The easiest identification is the **waxy green leaves, almost round and dime-to-quarter sized**, at 1.3–2 cm (1/2–3/4") across. Heavy veins give a ribbed look. **Leaves turn an attractive coppery-red in autumn**. Slim, brown catkins add further decoration.

Range: Carpets muskeg and damp sidehills in central and northern British Columbia but is very sporadic in Washington. San Juan Islands, Puget Sound, Columbia Gorge, lower eastern slopes of the Cascades. It turns up here and there to confound you. Not in the bunch-grass and sagebrush ecosystems.

LABRADOR TEA
Ledum groenlandicum

A shrub of **mossy, spongy bogs and wet, rocky side-hills**. Thin, twisting stems to 90 cm (3') tall carry **thick, narrow evergreen leaves that appear roughly whorled and have a rusty red wool beneath**. The leaf design is an effective way of conserving water. From May to July, depending on altitude, there will be **showy heads of white, star-like flowers**. Flowers have 5 petals and protruding stamens. They are followed by dry husks, which will hang on until next spring.

The *groenlandicum* part of the name reflects this shrub's occurrence in Greenland, but it ranges much further south. Native Americans of the eastern U.S. and Canada used the dried leaves for making a tea—a practice copied by early explorers and settlers. Though some tribes of the West used this plant for medicinal purposes and made a similar tea, it was never popular for tea in the West.

Range: Bogs of coast and mountain forest ecosystems. Puget Sound, Mt. Rainier.

TRAPPER'S TEA
Ledum glandulosum

A lthough slightly larger than Labrador tea, above, this shrub is quite similar except that the **evergreen leaves have a whitish wool on the underside**. Edges are slightly rolled over. White flowers have 5 petals and are 1.3 cm (1/2") across. Trapper's tea grows on **shady, damp mountainsides** where it forms a bushy tangle. The common name must be a misnomer, for the leaves contain a poisonous alkaloid. However, the plant has a pleasant fragrance.

Also known as: mountain Labrador tea.
Range: Most abundant east of the Cascades, on moist mountain slopes. Found up to 1500 m (5000'). Associated with black huckleberry and Engelmann spruce.

HARDHACK

Spiraea douglasii

Slender, reddish stems, usually about 1.2 m (4') tall, often forming a thicket. From May to August, each stem carries a **terminal pink plume of flowers**. This plume is 3 times as long as it is broad. In winter it becomes a very visible **pyramidal, brown husk**. Check by noting the oval, deciduous leaves, 5–7.5 cm (2–3") long. **Leaves are wooly on underside and have coarse notches on upper half of margin**.

Also known as: steeple bush, douglas spirea.

Range: Margins of ponds and wet meadows at low elevations throughout coast forest ecosystem. Also, mountains of Stevens County.

Douglas was generous in his range description, 'Northwest coast of America, about the Columbia and the Straits of Juan de Fuca.' He must have made his way through thickets of this shrub many times in his explorations—and with wet feet, for it favors wet, open places.

FLUFFY, PINKISH FLOWERS

LEAF

WINTER TWIG

SWEET GALE
Myrica gale

Almost always a shrubby, erect plant in the same habitat as hardhack, p. 118. Hard to see amidst a heavy growth of other shrubs. Slender stems to 1.2 m (4') tall carry thin, alternate, deciduous leaves. They are wedge-shaped, 1.3–5 cm (1/2–2'') long. **Upper third of leaf margin is coarsely notched. Leaf is dotted with yellow glands on top side and underside**. If crushed, the leaves release a fragrant scent. Clumps of greenish-yellow catkins appear before the leaves. These catkins change to brown, cone-like husks quite noticeable in winter.

Range: Margins of ponds, bogs and lakes west of the Cascades. Wet areas of the subalpine east of the Cascades. Circumboreal.

GREENISH
CATKINS

BIG SAGEBRUSH
Artemisia tridentata

This shrub **typifies the semi-arid regions of North America**. It survives where little else can. Height varies from 0.6 to 2.1 m (2'–7'). The **bushy form and sage-green color** are quickly recognizable. Crush a handful of leaves to smell a **spicy, tangy perfume**. Most **summer and autumn leaves are 3-toothed** but, in winter and spring, softer leaves without teeth appear at twig ends. They help to put on rapid growth when moisture is most abundant, then drop off to conserve moisture. Shallow, wide-spreading roots to absorb water quickly during rainstorms; others penetrate deeply to underground water. **Very small, drab flowers bloom** from mid-September to mid-October. **Almost always found on soils of volcanic origin**.

Range: The dominant growth over much of central and southeastern Washington, roughly the hottest and driest region. See it from the British Columbia border southward along the Okanogan River valley. Also southward from Wenatchee and the Grand Coulee area. Eastward from The Dalles on the Columbia River.

Lewis, April 20, 1806, '...for feul they [Native Americans] use straw, small willows and the southern wood [probably sagebrush, because a form of Artemisia *was known as 'southern wood' in the eastern states].'*

RIGID SAGEBRUSH
Artemisia rigida

Rigid sagebrush and big sagebrush, above, can be confused because of similar form and color. Rigid sagebrush often grows on even more **impoverished soils** than big sagebrush does, is usually **less than 60 cm (2') tall** and has a more rounded, compressed outline. Thick, twisted lower stems branch into short, stout spurs, hence the name 'rigid.' The **singly borne olive-green leaves appear to be in loose tufts**. A few leaves may fork. They measure to 4 cm (1 1/2") long. Often mixed with, or close to, big sagebrush.

Range: Appears sporadically, on dry benchlands and rocky slopes in eastern and central areas of the state. Grand Coulee, Vantage, Blue Mountains.

ANTELOPE-BRUSH

Purshia tridentata

An abundant shrub to 2.4 m (8') tall, with stiff, awkward branches. It is associated with sagebrush and the driest parts of the state. Overall, it has a dull green color, but during April and May it is **dotted with small, yellow flowers**. These flowers have a pleasant fragrance. The **leaves are triple notched or lobed** and are only 2.5 cm (1") long. You can drive for a long way along some interior routes and have antelope-brush as a constant companion.

Also known as: bitterbrush.

Range: Sagebrush and bunchgrass ecosystems. Tonasket to Brewster, Entiat, Leavenworth, Wenatchee, Ellensburg, Yakima, Pasco and eastward from The Dalles, Oregon.

Lewis recorded it in 1805, on the '...prairies of the Rocky-mountains and on the Columbia River.'

GREASEWOOD

Sarcobatus vermiculatus

Remember that **'dark green' is the key** to identifying this shrub, which grows to 1.8 m (6') tall. Among the olive-grays of the sagebrush community, the dark green of greasewood stands out clearly. But also check green rabbit-brush, p. 123. Further clues are that greasewood **favors alkaline areas**—look for a white, pasty substance on the ground—and the twig ends on lower limbs are spiny. **Leaves are fleshy and narrowly worm-like**, as the Latin word *vermiculatus* implies. A shrub carries **2 types of flowers** in the middle of summer. The male flower looks like a small catkin, the **female flower is a single bloom**. The fruit is an egg-shaped seed encircled by a papery wing. The botanical name provides no clue to the common name of greasewood. Possibly it burns with a greasy smoke.

Range: Sagebrush ecosystem. Coulee City to Ephrata, Vantage to Othello, Yakima, Pasco, Washtucna.

PRAIRIE SAGEWORT
Artemisia frigida

A shorter plant than others of the sagebrush community, at **less than 60 cm (2') tall**. Also note this plant's **softer, fringed appearance**. Crushed leaves have a **pungent sage smell. Leaves fork into 2–3 thin leaflets**. Small, dull flowers cluster along thin stems. Blooms in late summer.

Note: Botanically not a true shrub. *Artemisia* shrubs are on p. 120.

Range: Often with ponderosa pine. Okanogan and Ferry counties. Tonasket and eastward. Also known as: fringed sagebrush, pasture wormwood.

COMMON RABBIT-BRUSH
Chrysothamnus nauseosus

An attractive, **compact, olive-green shrub**. Although **often a part of the sagebrush scene**, it does favor less harsh conditions and so is more common on the upper fringes of pure sagebrush areas. It also readily expands into the ponderosa pine ecosystem. Averaging 0.6–1.2 m (2–4') in height, the many thin, branching stems are almost hidden by **long, string-thin, velvety leaves. Masses of small, yellow flowers adorn twig tips**.

Sometimes flowers are seen here and there as early as late July, but it is **usually late September before mass blooming occurs**. Jackrabbits browse on it—giving it its common name—and so do bighorn sheep and deer. Compare with gray horsebrush, p. 124.

Range: East of the Cascades, at upper edges of sagebrush areas. Okanogan and Chelan counties. Lyons Ferry (on Columbia River west of Starbuck), Vantage. Eastern part of Columbia Gorge.

GREEN RABBIT-BRUSH
Chrysothamnus viscidiflorus

The **key word is 'green'** for, except in color, this shrub is very similar to common rabbit-brush, above. Though this shrub is rather rare, it does stand out distinctly against the olive-gray coloration of the sagebrush community. Check against greasewood, p. 121, which is also green. Greasewood, however, is usually over 90 cm (3') tall and has spiny twig ends whereas this shrub is generally **less than 90 cm (3') tall** and has very thin leaves—possibly a little sticky, as the botanical name suggests. **Small, yellow flowers are in terminal clusters and in bloom into late summer**.

Range: Very similar to common rabbit-brush.

Douglas recorded it on the '...barren plains of the Columbia, from the Great Falls to mts.'

GRAY HORSEBRUSH
Tetradymia canescens

Another shrub similar in aspect to common rabbit-brush. The **2 key distinguishing features** to look for are **short leaves, about 1.3 cm (1/2") long**, and that **gray horsebrush blooms in June and early July—before common rabbit-brush**. Often this shrub is about 60 cm (2') tall and almost hidden in the more robust growth of big sagebrush. Twig-end clusters of 4–5 yellow flowers provide small bursts of color. **Each flower is held by 4 long, oblong bracts**.

Range: Sagebrush and bunchgrass ecosystems. Tonasket, Dry Falls, Vantage Highway.

DORR'S SAGE
Salvia dorii

A thick, shrubby growth to 50 cm (1 1/2') tall that looks **rather like a penstemon** (see pp. 114–15). Note the **many dozens of purplish flower stems** and **flowers with 2 long, projecting stamens and an even longer style**. Tiny flowers are in whorls, each supported by 2 small leaflets and broad, purplish bracts. Overall, it is a mass of bloom from April to June. The lower lip of the flower is a landing platform for a bee: the arching styles and stamens brush its back as it probes for nectar. The lower, twisting **limbs are sometimes covered with a crusty, orange substance**. Leaves numerous, opposite, paddle-shaped and mealy.

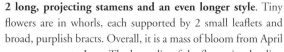

Also known as: purple sage.
Range: Dry, rocky soils. Often with rigid sagebrush. Sidehills around Vantage. Columbia Gorge east of The Dalles.

David Douglas collected seeds '...on the plains of the Columbia, near the Priest's Rapid [now Priest Rapids].'

HOP SAGE
Grayia spinosa

A shrub to 1.2 m (4') tall that usually escapes attention until it produces dabs of pinkish color from mid-May onward. Then it shows a wide and scattered distribution. Commonly it is a much-branched shrub about 60 cm (2') in height. Conspicuous in spring, when its twig ends display dense clusters of fruiting bracts tinged with pink and red. Twig ends also carry sharp spines—it is the only 'sagebrush' shrub with spines.

Also known as: spiny hopsage.
Range: Mostly in south-central sagebrush community, in Douglas, Yakima and Franklin counties. Grand Coulee, Yakima Canyon.

COMMON JUNIPER
Juniperus communis

To establish some of the importance of this sprawling green mat, let it be known that it is the most widely distributed shrub in the northern half of the world—it is circumpolar. It may be a tidy, upright clump of compact limbs or a sprawling carpet to 6 m (20') across. Other junipers are classed as trees, pp. 42–43. Narrow, sharp-pointed and 6 mm (1/4") long, the **needles have a whitish channel on the underside. Needles are arranged in whorls of three.** The fruit is a fleshy, knobby berry, dark blue to black and covered with a whitish bloom. Berries, although bitter and considered inedible, have had a great number of uses by northern peoples around the world. The one most often cited is for flavoring beer and gin.

Also known as: ground juniper.
Range: Wide altitudinal range, with a preference for dry, open slopes. Coastal in the San Juan Islands and Puget Sound. Mountain habitat in the Olympics and Coast Mountains.

WHITISH CHANNEL
LEAVES IN 3S
BERRY

POISON-IVY
Rhus radicans

Poison-ivy can be difficult to recognize because of its low, shrubby growth and the absence of showy flowers or berries. It mixes with other dryland plants and alerts you to its presence only by the **large, wavy-edged leaves in 3s**. Watch the base of rockslides, stony places and rocky road edges exposed to the sun. It often forms patches, usually not more than 60 cm (2') tall. It has a tough, twisting stem hidden by the leaves, which are glossy green until they turn red in the fall. In late spring, **small, white flowers** form clusters in the leaf axils. The **berries are round and whitish**.

All parts of the plant contain a toxic chemical that causes a severe skin irritation. Chamomile lotion is a standard remedy, as is washing with a strong soap. However, sheep, goats and cattle can graze on poison-ivy.

Range: Sagebrush, bunchgrass and lower elevations of ponderosa pine ecosystems. Okanogan, Ferry counties, Wenatchee, Yakima, Snake River.

LEAFLETS

BERRY

POISON-OAK
Rhus diversiloba

Another plant with **leaves in 3s. Leaves are glossy, leathery and variable in shape**. Some are lobed rather like an oak leaf. Can be a low, shrubby plant, a climber or an erect shrub to 1.5 m (5') tall. You will likely miss the tiny flowers in their loose cluster, but it is easier to notice the bunches of **greenish-white berries**. Like poison-ivy, poison-oak contains a chemical that causes itching. Treatment is the same.

Range: West side of Cascades, from Puget Sound southward. Inland along Columbia River into Klickitat County.

BERRIES

LEAFLETS

Note: Lewis and Clark and David Douglas never mentioned this plant, although they were often in the mid-Columbia Gorge, where it is abundant today. So, did they miss it, or did it not grow there in those days?

SMOOTH SUMAC
Rhus glabra

This shrub, with its crooked limb structure, up to 3 m (10') tall, usually grows in patches, by reason of long, sprouting roots. An arching **leaf has 13–21 leaflets**. In October, smooth sumac creates a **vivid red splash of color** on lower hillsides. Also by fall, the former clusters of pale greenish flowers have evolved into a **cone of red, plush-like seeds**. Roots, leaves and fruit were used by aboriginal peoples, later by herbalists.

Poison sumac, a similar plant, occurs in eastern U.S.

Range: A dryland shrub at lower elevations of the ponderosa pine ecosystem. Okanogan, Ferry, Chelan and Yakima counties. Snake River and tributaries.

13–21 LEAFLETS

SEED CONE

RED ELDERBERRY
Sambucus racemosa

Elderberries are **stout, upright shrubs** to 4.5 m (15') tall, with large compound leaves and **showy flower and berry clusters**. All elders have a large-diameter soft pith. The large, roundish clump of **small, yellowish-white flowers** blooms by early April. They have a faint but distinctive smell. Then there isn't much of an eye-catching display again until early June, when the berries tinge with red. By late June, the **berries are plump and bright red**. The head of berries is more or less upright. The opposite leaves carry 5–7 sharp-pointed, toothed leaflets; on a young shoot, leaves may have 9 leaflets.

The berries are edible after cooking, and coastal tribes once valued them. People 'in the know' can make very good jellies and wines from them.

Range: West of the Cascades, in shady bottomlands, along creeks and roadsides, from low to middle elevations. Columbia Gorge.

BLACK ELDERBERRY
Sambucus melanocarpa; S. racemosa var. *melanocarpa*

Sometimes recognized as a variety of the red species, above, black elderberry is seldom over 2.4 m (8') tall. Its **high mountain range** is a good indicator. Leaves have 5–7 leaflets. The flower cluster is rounded and loose. Berries are shiny and black. Blooms June to July.

Range: Mostly on eastern slopes of Cascades, from 900 m (3000') to timberline. Blue Mountains.

BLUE ELDERBERRY

Sambucus cerulea

Note that the similar red elderberry, p. 128, occurs in the coastal part of this one's range. A definite check is the number of leaflets, usually in 9s, versus the 5–7 of red elderberry. When in bloom, beginning in late May—after red elderberry—the **large, flat-topped flowerheads are distinctive**. But, for some strange reason, this shrub **produces flower clusters all summer**. The weight of the bluish berries, often with enough bloom to turn them whitish, can pull a head of berries down into a drooping position. The soft pith in the main stems was easily removed by the Native Americans, who found many uses for these natural tubes.

Range: Lower coastal slopes, but most abundant east of the Cascades. Stevens, Pend Oreille, Chelan, Yakima, Kittitas counties. Columbia Gorge.

Lewis, February 7, 1806, 'The Eder [blue elderberry] grows in great abundance in the rich woodlands this side of the Rocky mountains...the color of its being a pale sky blue.'

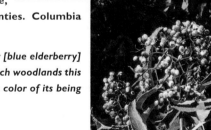

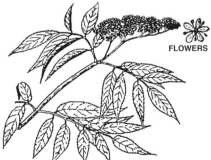

FLOWERS

129

WILD ROSES

Rosa spp.

Over 100 different species of wild roses are found in North America, but Washington State can claim fewer than 6. Each one displays white-to-deep-rose flowers with a fragrant perfume. The hips (fruit) hang on into winter. Leaves have an odd number of leaflets. Note that **native roses have straight spines and introduced roses have curved ones. Expect some confusion! A precise description seems impossible, even in the most learned source material**. But there is compensation nevertheless: *take time to smell the roses!*

NOOTKA ROSE

Rosa nutkana

The most common bush rose. Often forms thickets. To 3 m (10') tall, with **stout, straight thorns, usually paired**, at each leaf axil. **Leaves with 5–7 toothed leaflets**. Flowers mostly borne singly, May to July. Fruit is a showy scarlet hip, wider than tall.

Also known as: common wild rose.
Range: At lower elevations across the state, with 2 varieties.

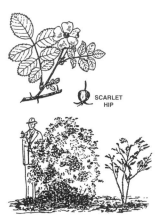

SCARLET HIP

BALDHIP ROSE

Rosa gymnocarpa

Slender stems bristly with weak, straight spines. There are 5-9 leaflets. Usually a single pale pink flower per twig end. **Orange hips lack sepals** and so are 'bald.'

HIP

Also known as: dwarf rose. **Range:** Widely distributed across the state in dry, coniferous woods, at low to middle elevations.

CLUSTERED WILD ROSE

Rosa pisocarpa

Armed with **straight spines, including a pair of larger ones at each leaf base.** Several small, pale flowers in a twig-end cluster. Fruit is pea-sized.

Also known as: swamp rose.
Range: Prefers swampy areas. Widespread at lower elevations west of the Cascades.

DOG ROSE

Rosa canina

Likely this is the white 'wild' rose that you will see occasionally. Usually it is a large, coarse shrub. The curved spines indicate that it is an import. Sometimes an old farm nearby suggests that it might be an escaped ornamental. Flowers are white to pink.

Range: Southern areas. Snake River, Steptoe Butte.

OREGON-GRAPE

Mahonia spp.

A ll 3 species of *Mahonia* are similar in having **ever-green, holly-like leaflets**. No other shrub resembles them, except for English holly, p. 80, an import that is sometimes found growing wild. Oregon-grape is a popular ornamental.

Also known as: Mahonia, holly grape.

CENTRAL VEIN

TALL OREGON-GRAPE

Mahonia aquifolium

This species is the one most commonly noticed, for it can be a twisting upright form to 1.5 m (5') tall and occasionally double that. The 7 (usually, but can be 5–9) **leaflets are a glossy dark green on both surfaces, with 1 central vein and spine-tipped** like English holly. **Clusters of bright yellow flowers** adorn the stems during May and June. They are followed by **dark blue berries with a whitish bloom**. They are ripe in August, but hang on until late fall. Their best use is in jellies and jams made using berries that are dead ripe or touched by frost. Frost may cause some of the leaves to turn red and be a decorative feature during winter. Native Americans used the yellow wood for making a yellow dye.

Range: Exposed situations with rocky soils, from low to middle elevations. San Juan Islands and Okanogan, Chelan, Yakima and Spokane counties.

DULL OREGON-GRAPE

Mahonia nervosa

The 2 key distinguishing features are **sprays of 9–19 leaflets** and **leaves dull green on both sides**. The 3 veins (hence *nervosa*), often given as a key, are indistinct. Usually a number of leaf sprays to a plant, which **averages 60 cm (2') in height**. Unlike the tall Oregon-grape, it has comparatively few yellow flowers. Berries are green to blue.

Range: Generally confined to lower elevations in open forests of coastal region.

CREEPING OREGON-GRAPE

Mahonia repens

Has **3–7 leaflets per leaf, each with 1 central vein; teeth short and weak. Leaves always dull beneath** and some with a whitish tinge. This plant may be almost flat on the ground or upright for 30 cm (1') or more.

Range: *East of the Cascades,* in open forests. Ellensburg, Wenatchee, Colville, Spokane, Pullman.

Clark, February 12, 1806, 'There are two species of evergreen shrubs, leaves....Each point of their crenate margins armed with a thorn or spine....I do not know the frute or flower of either.'

Lewis later collected seed of creeping Oregon-grape, and it was successfully grown in New York.

THIMBLEBERRY
Rubus parviflorus

Become familiar with this **unarmed** shrub, for you will see it again and again. It grows to 2.1 m (7') tall at the coast and to 75 cm (30") east of the Cascades. The leaves, flowers and berries are all quick identifying features. To 20 cm (8") across, the **large, soft green, velvety leaves have 3–7 lobes.** From May to late July, you may see **stark white, tissuey flowers**, 4 cm (1 1/2") across. Later, look for the soft and mushy, **raspberry-like fruit in a uniform dull red color.** The very attractive berries are not thimble-shaped, but are shallowly domed. Although edible, they are not greatly favored today except by birds and bears. People 'living off the land' long ago prepared these berries in various ways. The large leaves were used as food wrappers or to separate foods, the way we use wax paper or plastic wrap today.

Range: Often forms dense thickets along shady roadside areas, forest openings, stream and shoreline borders. Most abundant at lower elevations west of the Cascades, but found across the state in suitable habitats.

SALMONBERRY
Rubus spectabilis

Salmonberry and thimbleberry are grouped because in coastal areas they often occur together (and at times still puzzle me as to which name goes with which plant). Perhaps if you think of salmon (fish) as having reddish flesh, you can relate

salmonberry's name to the **reddish flowers** and the **berries that vary from yellow to red.** When you do not have leaves, flowers or berries as a guide, **note the golden-satiny stems with shredding bark.** Stems have scattered fine prickles and often form a dense thicket that springs from a branching root system. The erect, branching stems are 1.8–2.4 m (6–8') tall. A fresh green in color,

the **toothed leaves, bearing 3 sharply toothed leaflets,** appear in early April and are soon followed by attractive **light red, 5-petaled flowers** to 2.5 cm (1") across. Flowers may bloom well into July. The amber or reddish berries are edible, but soft. To Native Americans, the berries weren't nearly as important as the young stem sprouts harvested in early spring. These sprouts were peeled and eaten raw or steamed.

Range: West of the Cascades, in damp places below the subalpine.

Lewis, December 1, 1805, '...the broad leave shrub...has no joints, the leaf broad and deeply indented. The bark pals [peals] and hangs on the stem and is of a yellowish brown color.'

Douglas, April 19, 1825, as he and 6 Native Americans sat around a fire eating sturgeon, '...they [the Native Americans] ate young shoots of Rubus spectabilis....'

SASKATOON
Amelanchier alnifolia

Perhaps the name of a shrub evokes for you a cherished personal memory. For me, it goes back to childhood, springtime in the Okanagan in British Columbia and picking an immense bouquet of spring sunflowers (now less picturesquely known as balsamroot) and sprays of saskatoon. How much my mother appreciated this flamboyant, cumbersome collection, I don't remember.

A saskatoon on a rocky sidehill may be 2–4 m (6–12') tall. Often taller, but browsing by deer, elk or cattle can result in a misshapen shrub, just 1 m (3 1/2') tall. Usually a loose bush is formed, with upright limbs fanning outward—a shape recognizable from afar. The best identifying feature is the **small, rounded leaf, with regular notches on the upper half**, best seen on older leaves.

Clusters of 5-petaled, white blossoms, averaging 2 cm (3/4") across, liberally decorate this shrub during April and May. Don't confuse with mock-orange, p. 137. **Berries are a dull red by July and ripen to a reddish-purple or dark blue**. They are edible but not sought after to any degree in this region. Further east they are a favorite for jellies, syrups and pies. To the Native Americans the berries were an ingredient to be mixed with meat to make pemmican, a staple food. When dried, pemmican could be stored for months. Many tribes favored the tough, straight limbs for arrow-making.

Also known as: June berry, service berry.
Range: Widespread across the state. West of the Cascades it is generally below 600 m (2000'). Far more abundant in dry and rocky areas eastward. Often associated with ponderosa pine.

BEAKED HAZELNUT
Corylus cornuta var. *cornuta*

A many-stemmed open or bushy shrub to 3.7 m (12') tall. Without showy flowers or fruit, it is easily passed by. The **large, oval leaves with coarse toothing** make for good identification. Many shrubs have little or no fruit and likely you will have missed the conspicuous slender catkins of February and March. By July, the **nut is enclosed in a green, stocking-like husk** that blends perfectly with the leaves. The 'stocking' is about twice the length of the nut. The nuts are edible, but you face stiff competition from squirrels and Steller's jays.

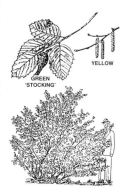

Range: **Lowlands and lower mountain slopes with open forest.**

CALIFORNIA HAZELNUT
Corylus cornuta var. *californica*

Similar to beaked hazelnut, above, but the **stocking is about the same length as the nut**.

Range: **Open coastal forests and east of the Cascades at upper edge of ponderosa pine areas. San Juan Islands. Kittitas and King counties. Chinook Pass.**

Clark, October 22, 1805, near The Dalles, '...we arrived at 5 Large Lod[g]es of natives...they gave us Philberts [hazelnuts]...and berries to eate.'

MOCK-ORANGE

Philadelphus lewisii

My vote for the shrub contributing the most floral beauty to the landscape. Mock-orange outshines all the others during May and into July, with a profusion of white blooms that last at least 2 months. Sometimes it is a small, limby shrub less than 1.8 m (6') tall perched on a rocky sidehill. On the coast, it is a more robust form to 4.5 m (15') tall. **White, 4-petaled blossoms to 2.5 cm (1") across** form in clusters and splash the shrub with eye-catching beauty. On the coast the flowers have a definite pleasant fragrance, but eastward they lack it. **Leaves, to 6.5 cm (2 1/2") long, are distinctive—note the 3 veins and the scattered pointed teeth on the leaf margins**. The new twigs have bright chestnut-brown bark, which often loosens as they age. Aboriginal peoples used the straight, tough stems for bows and arrows.

Also known as: syringa, bridal wreath.
Range: Often the dominant shrub on rocky slopes. Generally at lower elevations. Across the state, but favors the bunchgrass and ponderosa pine ecosystems. Coulee Dam, Dry Falls, Yakima, Spokane, Blue Mountains.

Lewis recorded this plant '...on the waters of Clarck's [Snake] river,' and its botanical name commemorates him.

Douglas collected seeds along the banks of the Columbia River.

OCEANSPRAY
Holodiscus discolor

Mock-orange, p. 137, may be the showiest and the longest blooming shrub, but oceanspray comes a close second. From May until the next spring, it is easily identified by the **plume of creamy white flowers, which persists over winter as a cluster of dried husks**. Individual flowers are very small, but mass together to form the lilac-like plumes. Seeing a row of oceanspray in full bloom on a steep roadside bank helps you appreciate its name. On the coast, this erect, several-stemmed plant may be 4.5 m (15') tall but, east of the Cascades, 1.8–2.4 m (6–8') is more common. **A distinctive leaf with a wedge-shaped base and coarse teeth**. Possibly Washington's most useful shrub, its exceedingly hard wood saw a wide variety of uses by Native American groups.

Range: From low to middle elevations, in open, dry locations across the state. Often in ponderosa pine and bordering forest regions. Ferry, Stevens and Spokane counties. Steptoe Butte and Kamiak Butte (near Palouse).

RED-OSIER DOGWOOD
Cornus stolonifera

Although lesss conspicuousness in thickets of willow, alder and water birch, red-osier dogwood has many noticeable and attractive features. In winter and early spring, the **thin stems are a shiny red**. In June, **round heads of small, white flowers** show up against the **dark green leaves with their 5–7 parallel veins**, as is common for all the dogwoods. By August, **the clumps of lead-white berries** are forming. Later, many **leaves turn a soft reddish-purple**.

Leaves are opposite. Side twigs and branches also form symmetrically. The bark of older wood, which generally fades to a dull brown, can vary in color. Mostly from 2–6 m (6 1/2–20') tall.

The long, flexible stems—ideal for constructing sweathouses, fish traps and fish-drying racks—had many uses by aboriginal groups. The bark was used for cordage. The berries, with their large seeds, had little value. Deer, elk and moose graze on twig ends.

Range: **Widespread, from lowlands to subalpine, in suitable habitats. Look for it along stream-courses and backwaters and in damp places.**

COMMON SNOWBERRY

Symphoricarpos albus

My guess is that snowberry, found anywhere from low to middle elevations, is the **shrub with the widest distribution** in the state. In fact, its thickets may be so commonplace that you don't notice them, especially when not bedecked with the **plump, waxy-white berries**. It may be growing against your back fence, bordering the local wooded park, as a thicket in an aspen grove or widely dispersed through an open mountainside forest. Usually not much more than 1.5 m (5') tall. **Tiny, pinkish flowers** form small clusters at twig ends during June and July. Prominent by early August, the **berries are sometimes considered poisonous** to humans, but coastal deer will seek them out. The opposite, deciduous leaves are untoothed; larger ones may be lobed.

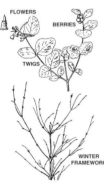

FLOWERS
BERRIES
TWIGS
WINTER FRAMEWORK

Also known as: waxberry.

Range: **Usually below 600 m (2000') at the coast, below 900 m (3000') east of the Cascades. Widespread, but not in bunchgrass or sagebrush ecosystems.**

TRAILING SNOWBERRY

Symphoricarpos mollis

Stems trail and grow roots. Sometimes forms the principal groundcover but is easily overlooked. Leaves, flowers and berries smaller than on the snowberry above.

Range: **San Juan Islands and coastal strip.**

PACIFIC NINEBARK
Physocarpus capitatus

Ninebarks receive their name from the supposedly 9 thin layers of shredding bark. **Older branches do have brown, shredding bark**, though young ones tend to be smooth. Look for this species in damp, open spaces, possibly with red-osier dogwood and thimbleberry nearby. Expect a rather dense, upright shrub 2–3.7 m (6 1/2–12') tall with arching branches. The distinctive leaves are alternate, with **3–5 sharp lobes**. In spring, the **rounded, white balls of tiny, 5-petaled flowers appear, with many pink stamens**. By mid-July these balls have become reddish clumps of rough seed husks.

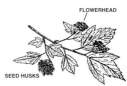

FLOWERHEAD

SEED HUSKS

Range: Damp, open lowlands west of the Cascades. Also in Columbia Gorge.

Lewis, February 7, 1806, 'The seven or ninebark...is also common in this quarter [Fort Clatsop].'

MALLOW NINEBARK
Physocarpus malvaceus

No confusion with Pacific ninebark, above, is likely, because mallow ninebark is found only east of the Cascades. Mostly stout and bushy, 0.6–1.2 m (2–4') tall. In September it is a bright russet-red and very noticeable on semi-open rocky hillsides. **Leaves are 3–5 lobed, mealy and palmately veined. Rounded masses of small, white flowers**, about 2.5 cm (1'') across, appear from late May into June. These flowers change to brown seed husks.

Range: An *abundant* shrub on roadsides, hillsides, *east of the Cascades*. **Often with ponderosa pine and Douglas-fir. Ferry, Stevens and Pend Oreille counties. Blue Mountains.**

REDSTEM CEANOTHUS

Ceanothus sanguineus

A nondescript, ragged shrub 0.6–1.8 m (2–6') tall, it does have red stems. As with all ceanothuses, the **leaves have 3 main veins**. They are deciduous, finely toothed and about 4 cm (1 1/2") long. In June, there are masses of **small, fine-scented, white flowers**. The hard seed pods persist until next spring and are an identifying clue for several months. Look for this shrub with Douglas maple, oceanspray, saskatoon and snowbrush. This shrub is heavily browsed by deer and elk.

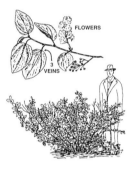

Range: Scattered occurrences west of Cascades, but abundant to the east, especially in northeastern counties. Also in Blue Mountains.

DEERBRUSH

Ceanothus integerrimus

Deerbrush may have **white flowers or pale to deep-blue ones**. Shrubs with different blossom colors may be right next to each other, and you could easily think that you have found 2 different shrubs—but they are really the same basic shrub. Tiny **flowers have a sweet fragrance** and form loose plumes 5–15 cm (2–6") long. They evolve into dry capsules, each with a hard seed.

This loosely branched shrub has slender, spreading, greenish limbs. It ranges from 1.2 to 2.4 m (4–8') tall. To 5 cm (2") long, the narrow, oval **leaves have the characteristic 3 veins** of *Ceanothus* spp.

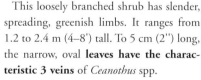

Range: East of the Cascades, from Yakima County southward, in exposed to partly shady places; roadsides, rockslides and dry forests at lower elevations.

SNOWBRUSH
Ceanothus velutinus

An **abundant** shrub, common along many mountain forest roads. Bushy and sprawling, to 1.5 m (5') tall, with smooth limbs that branch and twist outward and upward. About 5 cm (2") long, the **thick evergreen leaves have a glossy but gummy upper surface and are soft and velvety beneath; they have 3 veins**, as is typical of *Ceanothus* spp. During June, large, soft heads of tiny flowers cover the topmost branches and fill the air with a **pleasant scent**. Flowers may be seen until late August. Seeds may lie on the ground for years until a fire stimulates them to germinate. Mixing some flowers with water makes a soapy lather. Some Native Americans used the leaves as tobacco.

Also known as: buckbrush, sticky laurel.
Range: Infrequent west of the Cascades, but common eastward. Often a part of the Douglas-fir and ponderosa pine regions. Seen on eastern slopes of high passes in the Cascades. Blue Mountains.

Douglas found it at the 'Kettle Falls' (now flooded) on the Columbia River.

Today, it is difficult to visualize the problems of a plant collector in Douglas's time. To preserve them for study, plants had to be arranged on a sheet of paper and labeled, and notes made. Usually the paper had to be changed to complete the drying process. Newspapers certainly weren't locally available—in fact, paper for any purpose had to be brought from England. Special paper was carried in an oilcloth to protect it from moisture. And, for weeks at a time, there could be almost continual rain. Douglas was almost always on the move, which involved travel that started at daybreak and usually ended at dusk.

BLACK TWINBERRY
Lonicera involucrata

A sturdy shrub, 0.9–3 m (3–10') tall, usually mixed with low willows, red-osier dogwood and salmonberry. Suddenly, in July or August, you may encounter a floral-like design so unusual that it will stick in your memory. The common name is a direct help to identification if you see it—2 plump, shiny black berries encircled by a maroon-colored cape consisting of 4 bracts. This eye-catching decoration is preceded, some time from April to June, by twin yellow flowers 1.3 cm (1/2") long. The opposite, light green leaves are 5–15 cm (2–6") long. Though attractive, the berries are considered inedible.

TWIN-FLOWERS   CAPE   TWIN-BERRY

Also known as: bearberry honeysuckle.
Range: Damp places, streamside thickets. Low elevations to about 900 m (3000'). Most abundant west of the Cascades. Olympics, Cascades and other mountain systems. Western part of Columbia Gorge.

UTAH HONEYSUCKLE
Lonicera utahensis

A shrub from 0.6 to 1.5 m (2–5') tall that produces a spray of straggly branches with dry, peeling bark. Though somewhat variable in shape, the thin, round, opposite leaves are characteristic of the honeysuckles. Distinctive twin creamy flowers about 1.3 cm (1/2") long may appear as early as May at lower elevations. As each pair of jelly-like, red berries develops, 1 berry often grows much larger at the expense of the other. There is no information available on edibility or medicinal uses.

Also known as: red twinberry.
Range: Generally east of the Cascades, in moist forests from low elevations to the edge of the subalpine. Spokane and Blue Mountains.

143

GOATSBEARD
Aruncus dioicus

R eally not a shrub, because this plant dies to the ground each year. However, because of its vigorous growth, likely would be taken for a shrub. This 1–2 m (3–7') tall plant has **many pencil-like strings of very small, white flowers**. Male and female flowers are on separate plants. Although the **'pencils' hang on all summer**, they are best seen during May and June, before they turn a dirty brown. The stem of each long, lower leaf divides into 3 branchlets. Each branchlet usually carries 5 sharply toothed leaflets. The roots were used by Native American peoples to treat a wide variety of ills.

LEAFLET

Range: Streamsides, roadsides and forest edges that are shady and damp. A common roadside plant in northern Washington.

BIRCH-LEAVED SPIREA
Spiraea betulifolia

C ould be taken for a wildflower, but it does have a woody stem, slender and to 60 cm (2') tall. Usually, it is a **dense, flat-topped crown of small, white flowers** that catches the attention. Flowers may be tinged with pink. Leaves are distinctive once you see them several times, for they are to 6.5 cm (2 1/2") long and the **upper two-thirds of each leaf has a coarsely toothed margin**. Don't confuse with shrubby saskatoon, p. 135.

FLOWER HEAD

Note: For a pink spirea of the subalpine, p. 152.

Also known as: flat-top spirea.
Range: East of the Cascades, at low to middle elevations, in dry, open forests. Bunchgrass and ponderosa pine ecosystems.

PYRAMID SPIREA

Spiraea pyramidata

Usually a slim, erect shrub 0.5–1 m (1 1/2–3 1/2') in height, easily overlooked if it wasn't for the **pyramidal plume of white or pinkish flowers**. This plume, to 10 cm (4") tall, consists of tiny 5-petaled flowers. Blooms from late May to August. The oval leaves are to 7.5 cm (3") long and, as with birch-leaved spirea, p. 144, the top two-thirds of each is irregularly toothed along the margin.

FLOWER HEAD

Range: East of the Cascades, in open sunny areas below 1350 m (4400') elevation. Douglas-fir and ponderosa pine regions. Kittitas County, Cle Elum, Yakima.

SOOPOLALLIE

Shepherdia canadensis

In summer, upper twigs are covered with **clusters of translucent bright red berries**. Note the dark green leaves, roughly egg-shaped and 2.5–6.5 cm (1–2 1/2") long. The leaf **undersurface has silvery hairs and rusty brown spots**. Twigs have the same spotting. The **small, yellowish, 4-petaled flowers**, slightly different male and female versions on separate bushes, usually go unnoticed.

Soopolallie berries, when whipped or rubbed and mixed with water, produce a froth euphemistically known as 'Indian ice-cream.'

BERRIES

Also known as: soapberry, Canada buffaloberry. **Range:** Mostly east of the Cascades, but sporadic in San Juan Islands and Olympics. *Favors dry, open Douglas-fir forests.*

145

DEVIL'S CLUB
Oplopanax horridus

O *plopanax* signifies that this species is an armed plant of the ginseng family. If you unexpectedly encounter it, you might suspect that *horridus* is Latin for 'ouch, ouch.'

Generally, a sprawling shrub, 1.2–2.1 m (4–7') tall, with noticeably large leaves to 35 cm (14") across. The leaves are the largest of any shrub in the state and are arranged to maximize the amount of leaf surface exposed to the dim light beneath the forest canopy.

The cluster of small, white-greenish flowers just above the leaves usually goes unnoticed. By middle to late summer, the cluster has transformed into a showy cone of bright red berries. They are considered inedible, but black bears have a taste for them.

The name of devil's club seems very appropriate if you have the misfortune to grab a stem to steady yourself. Long, yellow, spiny bristles cover the stems and the undersides of the leaves. Easily detached from the plant, they usually cause festering if not removed from the skin.

Especially in coastal areas, devil's club could have rated as the most important medicinal plant to the aboriginal peoples. Arthritis and diabetes were only 2 of the ailments treated. The roots and the greenish inner bark provided the most potent medicines—and still have similar uses today. Different Native American groups had their own means of preparing wood and bark for drinks and poultices. The soft, easily carved wood was used in making fishing lures. With so much power attributed to this shrub, it might well be scientifically investigated for its medicinal properties.

Range: Lower elevations in coastal areas, along streams or on wet ground. Often associated with western redcedar and skunk cabbage.

Neither Lewis nor Clark made particular mention of this plant in their journals, although it was most surely brought to their attention.

Just before leaving England on October 27, 1829, Douglas wrote to Hooker, 'I cannot tell you how pleased I am to have the first part [of] your 'Flora Boreali—Americana' before sailing....The map is good....The plates are truly beautiful.'

SCOTCH BROOM

Cytisus scoparius

Not a native shrub, but so prolific and showy in the San Juans and Puget Sound that it is included here. Seeds were brought from Hawaii to southern Vancouver Island in the early 1850s by Captain Walter Colquhoun Grant, an early settler in Sooke, British Columbia. From the 3 seeds that germinated, it spread rapidly. Once a prized ornamental, it now crowds out more desirable native vegetation. Their slender, unarmed, green stems create a massed growth to 1.8 m (6') tall. From May to July, broom forms a **mass of bright yellow blooms**—its **flowers are typical for the pea family** and stick out from the stems at all angles. By July, most bushes are hung thickly with small, **black 'pea pods.'** On hot days they crack open with easily heard

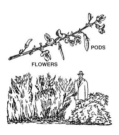

snaps. Pods and seeds should not be eaten, because of toxic qualities. The introduced broom is a serious weed pest here and is very difficult to eradicate.

Range: Roadsides and waste places throughout western Washington.

GORSE

Ulex europaeus

An introduced shrub that **resembles broom**, above, in its shrubby green form and yellow 'pea' flowers. Flowers are out before those of other shrubs—as early as January. Usually sprawling and less than 1.2 m (4') tall. It has **small, spiny leaves**.

Range: Exposed coastal areas and dry meadows. San Juan Islands and southward along Puget Sound. West side of Olympic Peninsula.

BUSH LUPINE
Lupinus arboreus

The word *arboreus* suggests 'tree-like,' and this lupine is indeed the **largest lupine** that you will ever see! This many-stemmed, bushy shrub, to 1.8 m (6') tall, is thickly covered with **lupine leaves bearing 5–11 leaflets**. Showy **yellow 'pea' flowers form long, twig-end sprays**. Considering its size and lupine leaves, there is no other shrub with which to confuse it.

Also known as: tree lupine.
Range: Appears to favor areas close to the ocean. San Juan Islands. Anacortes, Port Townsend. Southward to California.

HAIRY MANZANITA
Arctostaphylos columbiana

A rather low 'hide-away' shrub without prominent flowers or berries. But on the edge of a cliff or growing on a rocky outcrop, its twisting, reddish-brown branches and dull green leaves give it a character that only a dwarfed arbutus, p. 48, can copy. Usually rounded or sprawling in form, it is **seldom over 1.8 m (6') tall**. The **small, urn-shaped flowers are in clusters at twig ends**. The following **mealy, blackish-red berries** were gathered by aboriginal peoples and eaten either raw or cooked but are seemingly disregarded by all today. *Manzanita* is Spanish for 'little apple' and refers to the fruit.

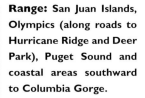

Range: San Juan Islands, Olympics (along roads to Hurricane Ridge and Deer Park), Puget Sound and coastal areas southward to Columbia Gorge.

SALAL
Gaultheria shallon

Possibly the coastal forest's most abundant shrub. It varies from a low, sparse
growth to an impenetrable tangle of twisting,
interlocking stems 3 m (10') or more tall.
Strong winds or occasional heavy snows do
no damage. **Leaves are alternate, evergreen,
thick and leathery**, egg-shaped and finely
toothed.

Bell or urn-shaped flowers hang bead-like
along the twigs and are seen from mid-May to
July. By August, the **plump, blackish-purple
berries** are ripening. The name salal comes to
us from coastal Native American groups for
whom the shrub provided a plentiful and
dependable food. The mealy berries were
eaten fresh, turned into a syrup or dried into
cake form. They were used as a sweetener for
other foods or mixed in to add flavor. Today,
we know that the berries make excellent jams
and jellies. Deer and bear also eat them. Cut
sprays of the dark green leaves are long lasting and thus
favored by florists. Salal is popular for planting around new
construction or damaged areas. It is becoming a popular plant
for horticultural nurseries, where it is raised from cuttings.

Range: Generally west of the Cascades, at lower elevations. San Juan Islands, Olympics and southward along
coastal strip to Columbia Gorge.

*Clark, December 9, 1805, '...an old woman presented [in] a
bowl...a kind of Surup made of dried berries which is common
to this Country which the natives Call Shele wele this surup I
thought was pleasant....'*

*Lewis, February 4, 1806, '...the Elk...feed on grass and rushes...in the woody country their
food is huckleberry bushes, fern, and an evergreen shrub [salal]...constitutes the greater
part of their food and grows abundantly through all the timbered country.'*

*Lewis, February 8, 1806, 'The Shallon...generally rises to a height of 3 feet. It grows very
thick...this shrub is an evergreen...the fruit is a deep purple berry.'*

INDIAN PLUM
Oemleria cerasiformis

Identifies itself in the coastal shrub complex by being the **first shrub to show bright green leaves**, sometimes by late February. Usual form is a several-stemmed, open shrub to 4.5 m (15') tall, bushy and erect in the open, sprawling in the shade. From each cluster of leaves, **4–9 small, white flowers hang**, in various stages of opening. Flowers, broken bark and crushed leaves have a peculiar odor. By May, the berries are well formed and have a dramatic **yellow-to-peach color** and look like small apricots. **Berries ripen to a bluish-black,** like small plums, with a deep white bloom. Though the berries consist of thin, tasteless rinds over large, hard pits, they saw some food use by Native Americans.

Also known as: oso-berry, skunk bush.
Range: San Juan Islands and low coastal forest west of Cascades.

PACIFIC RHODODENDRON
Rhododendron macrophyllum

The **state flower of Washington!** And a magnificent floral tribute it makes, appearing as shrubs to 3 m (10') tall, with **glossy evergreen leaves** setting off **large clusters of pinkish-rose flowers**. It blooms from May to June, with flower bunches to 15 cm (6") or more across. Flowers have 5 lobes rather than 5 distinct petals. The **10 long, curving, pink stamens** add to the floral design. Usually in groups, this shrub favors forest borders and road edges, and so contributes to public display. **Form is much like cultivated rhododendrons**, but with a tendency to open up and sprawl when under a forest canopy. It is protected by law from roadside cutting.

Also known as: California rhododendron.
Range: San Juans and coastal ecosystem. Olympics—southeastern flank. Sequim, Whidbey Island, Coupeville, Seattle, western part of Columbia Gorge.

WHITE-FLOWERED RHODODENDRON
Rhododendron albiflorum

Try and push through great tangles of this shrub's limbs and see why bushwhacking hikers call it 'mountain misery.' A low shrub, 0.9–1.8 m (3–6') tall, of high mountains. **Rough whorls of 5–7 thin, deciduous leaves** might be confused with copperbush (below) or false azalea (p. 152). Turn a leaf to catch the light and look closely at the top surface to see **fine coppery hairs**. Also, the **large, white flowers are almost 2.5 cm (1") across**, double the size of those on copperbush; false azalea has tiny, coppery bells.

Also known as: white rhododendron.
Range: From 1050 m (3500') elevation to near timberline on coastal slopes. Shady, moist places in Cascades and Olympics. Clallum County, Stevens Pass, Mt. Rainier, Mt. Adams.

COPPERBUSH
Cladothamnus pyroliflorus

A not-too-common shrub of coastal forests above 750 m (2500') elevation. It mingles with white rhododendron and false azaleas to create a brushy understory 0.9–1.5 m (3–5') in height. Identify it by finding its **stout stems with loose, coppery bark**. A **fine, waxy powder makes the leaves a paler green** than on neighboring plants. Although they are alternate, it is more important that the **leaves are in a rough whorl pattern**. They are 2.5–5 cm (1–2") long and the veins are very prominent.

During June and July it bears **pink-coppery flowers**, usually single and to 1.3 cm (1/2") across, each with a **protruding curved stigma**. A bumpy, green capsule replaces the flower.

Range: Damp areas in high forests west of the Cascades. Usually with mountain hemlock. Subalpine elevations in Olympics.

FALSE AZALEA
Menziesia ferruginea

This shrub's **height of up to 1.8 m (6')**, its erect, limby framework and its **small leaves in rough whorls** are quite similar to those of white rhododendron, copperbush and black huckleberry. Notice the **bluish-green leaves, to 5 cm (2") long**, and look for a little spine at the tip of the central vein. Leaves may carry rusty hairs. Young twigs are often covered with fine hairs. Small, bell-shaped flowers are an unusual pale coppery color. They have 4 petals and 4 sepals. Later, instead of berries, you will find dry, inedible capsules—perhaps the reason for the name 'fool's huckleberry.' Leaves turn an attractive orange-red in autumn.

Also known as: fool's huckleberry.
Range: Moist slopes, from 700 m (2300') to subalpine. Olympics. Both slopes of Cascades. Mt. Rainier, Stevens Pass, Skamania County.

SUBALPINE SPIREA
Spiraea densiflora

A trim and colorful shrub when in bloom. Makes its home on **high, open mountain slopes**, where it may be a bushy shrub or even a small thicket, usually not over 90 cm (3') tall. Very leafy, with oval leaves to 5 cm (2") long. **Tiny, pink-to-red flowers in massed heads** to 4 cm (1 1/2") across bloom during August.

Also known as: pink spirea.
Range: Subalpine meadows. Olympics, Cascades, Blue Mountains. Paradise Visitor Center at Mt. Rainier.

SITKA MOUNTAIN-ASH

Sorbus sitchensis

Most people recognize a mountain-ash if it is carrying its coral-red berries, for there are several similar and popular ornamental species. Native mountain-ash appears as **shrubby growths on the higher mountains**. Their colorful autumn bunches of red berries are displayed more prominently after the leaves have fallen. This shrub can be a sparse, slender-stemmed shrub to 2.4 m (8') tall or a brushy thicket. Usually it is found in the open.

The compound **leaf has 7–11 round-tipped leaflets with coarse teeth two-thirds of the way from tip to base**. During June, watch for **tiny, white flowers in round-topped clusters** 5–10 cm (2–4''). The **bright red berries** are at their finest during September, but hang on into October. They have a sour taste and mealy texture, but some people know how to make a jelly from them.

Range: General distribution throughout mountain and subalpine ecosystems. Most abundant above 1050 m (3500') in Cascades. Mt. Baker, Chinook Pass. Spotty occurrence in the Olympics and Blue Mountains.

WESTERN MOUNTAIN-ASH

Sorbus scopulina

Very similar to the mountain-ash above, but has **9–13 sharp-pointed, yellowish-green leaflets, with teeth almost the entire length of the margin**. Flower clusters are usually less than 5 cm (2'') across. **Shiny orange-to-scarlet berries** follow in late summer and into autumn.

Range: Mostly on western slopes of Cascades. Common in Olympics and Stevens Pass and on Mt. Rainier and Mt. Adams.

REFERENCES

Brayshaw, T. C. *Trees and Shrubs of British Columbia*. Vancouver: University of British Columbia Press, 1996.

Davies, John. *Douglas of the Forests: the North American Journals of David Douglas*. Seattle: University of Washington Press, 1980.

Douglas, C. W., G. B. Straley and D. Meidinger. *The Vascular Plants of British Columbia*. Special Report Series 1–4. Victoria: British Columbia Ministry of Forests, Research Branch, 1990–94.

Hawke, David Freeman. *Those Tremendous Mountains*. New York: Norton, 1980.

Hitchcock, C. L., A. Cronquist, M. Ownbey and J. W. Thompson. *Vascular Plants of the Pacific Northwest*. Parts 1–5. Seattle: University of Washington Press, 1955, 1959, 1961, 1964, 1969.

Hosie, R. C. *Native Trees of Canada*. Don Mills: Fitzhenry and Whiteside, 1979.

Kirk, Ruth, and Camelia Alexander. *Exploring Washington's Past: A Road Guide to History*. Seattle: University of Washington Press, 1990.

Lyons, C. P. *Trees, Shrubs and Flowers to Know in British Columbia*. Vancouver: J. M. Dent & Sons, 1956.

———. *Wildflowers of Washington*. Edmonton: Lone Pine Publishing, 1997.

Lyons, C. P., and Bill Merilees. *Trees, Shrubs and Flowers to Know in British Columbia and Washington*. Edmonton: Lone Pine Publishing, 1995.

Morwood, William. *Traveler in a Vanished Landscape; the Life and Times of David Douglas*. New York: C. N. Potter, 1973.

Parish, Roberta, Ray Coupé and Dennis Lloyd. *Plants of Southern Interior British Columbia*. Edmonton: Lone Pine Publishing, 1996.

Peattie, Donald Culross. *A Natural History of Western Trees*. Boston: Houghton Mifflin Co., 1950.

Pojar, Jim, and Andy MacKinnon. *Plants of the Pacific Northwest Coast*. Edmonton: Lone Pine Publishing, 1994.

Thwaites, Reuben G., ed. *Original Journals of the Lewis and Clark Expedition, 1804–1806*. 8 vols. 1904–05. Reprint. New York: Arno Press, 1969.

Turner, N. J. 1975. *Food Plants of British Columbia Indians*. Victoria: Royal British Columbia Museum.

Willard, Terry. 1992. *Edible and Medicinal Plants of the Rocky Mountains and Neighboring Territories*. Calgary: Wild Rose College of Natural Healing.

INDEX

INDEX

ABOUT THE AUTHOR

The mountains and streams were only minutes away from the family orchard in British Columbia's Okanagan Valley where Chess Lyons spent his boyhood. The Depression years offered little money for recreation, but hiking, camping and fishing were for the taking.

Chess graduated from the University of British Columbia with a degree in Forest Engineering. In 1940 he became the first technical employee of the newly formed Parks Branch of the B.C. Forest Service. In the next 10 years, either by himself or with another forester, Mickey Trew, he explored a number of vast, virtually unknown wilderness parks and the first park plans were formulated. Among these provincial parks were Tweedsmuir, Wells Gray, Manning and Kokanee Glacier. Other explorations resulted in more large parks being established, such as Muncho Lake, Liard River Hotsprings and Stone Mountain, all along the Alaska Highway.

Later, while he was in charge of historic sites in British Columbia, he was responsible for the first four years of the restoration of Barkerville, the historic gold-mining town in central British Columbia. Leaving government service after 22 years, Mr. Lyons then produced wildlife and travel films for the National Audubon Society and The World Around Us travel series. He gave over 1000 lecture and film presentations. With this background, he acted as a tour guide on trips to over one dozen countries.

Trees, Shrubs and Flowers to Know in British Columbia, written by Mr. Lyons and published in 1952, was the first non-technical field guide to plants for the province. He brought out a similar book for Washington two years later. They served for four decades, but were eventually updated and combined into *Trees, Shrubs and Flowers to Know in Washington and British Columbia*, which was released in 1995. A color field guide, *Wildflowers of Washington*, by C.P. Lyons, was produced in 1997.

The author's ingrained love of travel and interest in history and nature is reflected in the fact that, he traveled some 580,000 km (360,000 mi)—from the Pacific to the Atlantic and from Alaska to Guatemala—in his small Toyota-based Chinook camper. Washington State, with its easy access from B.C., its diversity of history and scenery and an intriguing network of backwoods roads, was an attraction for many years.

On many of his travels Mr. Lyons found himself on routes that had been used by the pioneering explorer-botanists Meriwether Lewis, William Clark and David Douglas. His curiosity about these pioneers led to a study of their journals, which documented their travels and botanizing. By sharing some of his findings in this book, Mr. Lyons hoped to add a touch of history and adventure to the wealth of trees and shrubs found in Washington State.

More Great Books about the Outdoors

Wildflowers of Washington, by C.P. Lyons
ISBN 1-55105-092-7 • 5.5" x 8.5" • 192 pages • $15.95 US

From seashore to mountain peak, the wild, untended blossoms of Washington flourish throughout the season. Lavish color photos and complete descriptions of over 500 species of wildflowers make this an essential companion on your next hike or picnic.

Birds of the Pacific Northwest Coast, by Nancy Baron & John Acorn
ISBN 1-55105-082-X • 5.5" x 8.5" • 240 pages • $15.95 US

This book describes more than 200 of the most common birds along the Pacific Northwest coast from Alaska through British Columbia and Washington to Oregon. Full-color illustrations throughout help enhance your enjoyment of the rich variety of bird life in this area.

Plants of the Pacific Northwest Coast: Washington, Oregon, British Columbia & Alaska, by Jim Pojar & Andy MacKinnon
ISBN 1-55105-040-4 • 5.5" x 8.5" • 528 pages • $19.95 US

An easy-to-use field guide featuring 794 species of plants commonly found along the Pacific coast from Oregon to Alaska, including trees, shrubs, wildflowers, aquatic plants, grasses, ferns, mosses and lichens. Covers the coastal region from shoreline to alpine, including the western Cascades. Features 1100 color photos, more than 1000 line drawings and silhouettes, clear species descriptions of each plant's habitat and range, and 794 color range maps.

Seashore of the Pacific Northwest, by Ian Sheldon
ISBN 1-55105-161-3 • 4.25" x 8.25" • 192 pages • $11.95 US

A spectacular guide to the Pacific Northwest's intertidal life with full-color illustrations of 150 species. Concise descriptions of mammals, fish, snails, worms, seaweeds and more. Pocket-sized with color-coded tabs.

Canadian Orders	US Orders
Phone 1-800-661-9017	Phone 1-800-518-3541
Fax 1-800-424-7173	Fax 1-800-548-1169

Visit our website at <www.lonepinepublishing.com>.